Food Truck Business

How to Start a Mobile Food Business the Easy Way

(Everything You Need to Know to Start Your Food Truck Business)

Eleanor Rivers

Published By **Zoe Lawson**

Eleanor Rivers

All Rights Reserved

Food Truck Business: How to Start a Mobile Food Business the Easy Way (Everything You Need to Know to Start Your Food Truck Business)

ISBN 978-1-77485-532-4

No part of this guidebook shall be reproduced in any form without permission in writing from the publisher except in the case of brief quotations embodied in critical articles or reviews.

Legal & Disclaimer

The information contained in this ebook is not designed to replace or take the place of any form of medicine or professional medical advice. The information in this ebook has been provided for educational & entertainment purposes only.

The information contained in this book has been compiled from sources deemed reliable, and it is accurate to the best of the Author's knowledge; however, the Author cannot guarantee its accuracy and validity and cannot be held liable for any errors or omissions. Changes are periodically made to this book. You must consult your doctor or get professional medical advice before using any of the suggested remedies, techniques, or information in this book.

Upon using the information contained in this book, you agree to hold harmless the Author from and against any damages, costs, and expenses, including any legal fees potentially resulting from the application of any of the information provided by this guide. This disclaimer applies to any damages or injury caused by the use and application, whether directly or indirectly, of any advice or information presented, whether for breach of contract, tort, negligence, personal injury, criminal intent, or under any other cause of action.

You agree to accept all risks of using the information presented inside this book. You need to consult a professional medical practitioner in order to ensure you are both able and healthy enough to participate in this program.

Table Of Contents

Introduction 1

Chapter 1: Why Should You Choose The Food Truck? 4

Chapter 2: Different Types 15

Chapter 3: The Importance Of Having A Plan Is The Most Important Thing 22

Chapter 4: Finding The Right Medium 40

Chapter 5: The Topic Is Money 63

Chapter 6: Learn The Rules 75

Chapter 7: Team 84

Chapter 8: Marketing 89

Chapter 9: Menu 101

Chapter 10: The Tenth Chapter: Grow . 114

Chapter 11: Management And Hiring .. 124

Chapter 12: How To Survive In 136

Chapter 13: The Subject Is Marketing .. 141

Chapter 14: Monitor Costs 160

Chapter 15: A Mistake To Avoid 175

Chapter 16: Food Safety Guidelines 178

Conclusion 183

Introduction

when we are talking about the entire mobile food vending business There are a variety of terms that are thrown around. Some of these terms are used interchangeably even when they are actually referring to slightly different things. When you're beginning to build a few thoughts about the specs of your food truck, it is important to be as precise as you can about your plans the goals you're aiming for, as well as the kind of food truck you're looking for. Let's examine a few various models of food vendors that fall under"the "food truck" umbrellaso that you'll get an idea of which will work best for your requirements. The first classification you'll need to know is "restricted" versus "unrestricted.""Restricted" means that the mobile food vendor is only licensed to sell food that has already been prepared and packaged. Some examples include ice-cream truck, which offer individually wrapped ice cream items as well as "roach coaches."Restricted food companies do not prepare food on site and simply keep food cold or warm and then distribute the items when they're ordered. "Unrestricted" implies that the food is cooked to be cooked, served, and sold through the vehicle. In general they have the home base or commissary they depend on to clean, replenish, and routine maintenance. "Unrestricted" is actually an overstatement as there are many rules and regulations that apply to these kinds of vehicles. In this publication, we'll mostly concentrate on the rules for a non-restricted company but there will be pertinent information for anyone who is interested about the mobile-food industry.

Despite those requirements There are a variety of alternatives to take your food with you on the go. Below , we'll discuss the various types capacities, specifications, and specifications for mobile food vending machines. In each class there are a lot of variations. The great thing about having your restaurant open out on the road is that you'll have the option of modifying your restaurant to suit your needs Be aware that these are generalizations. Let's look at these specifications when we dive deeper into the design and function specifics. At this point in the process of planning the main priority is narrowing down specific aspects by a small amount at one time.

Chapter 1: Why Should You Choose The Food Truck?

Food truck business is one of the fastest growing businesses across the US. There are many reasons you should incorporate the use of a food truck in your food service. Let us enumerate it:

Quick Start-Up

In the event of integrating food trucks into your establishment, initial setup generally takes less time than the traditional method of launching your store. Food trucks are available to lease at any time and it is possible to locate a vendor that is willing to lend a truck you. If you require additional trucks to serve customers or for your restaurant, you can lease additional units for less than establishing a brand new restaurant by starting from scratch.

Competitive Food

If you're looking to compete with other eateries in your local area, it could be the right choice for you as it will be able to compete in areas that are crowded. Food trucks will definitely offer a distinct selling point that will distinguish it from other food trucks by offering quick and easy access to services, particularly in peak times.

Budget Operation Low Budget Operation

The operation of a food truck is extremely flexible, and does not require much money to invest. When compared to dining establishments it is a lot less expensive to start food trucks and their upkeep is usually low. This is particularly beneficial for those who are new to the industry, since the financial risk is very low.

High Mobility

The secret to earning money in this industry is to "be in the same place your customers are" thus, the mobility of your company is essential. In contrast to restaurants with heavy machinery and slow services A food truck is able to serve customers much faster. It is also able to be moved according to the demands of the business. Since the majority of truck drivers are employees it allows for a more personal approach to business, particularly if you are planning to drive your own truck.

Mobile Branding

Food trucks are an excellent way to advertise your company's image. If you are able to attract prospective customers to your company with the food trucks, chances are that they'll be aware of your other ventures and will be to your food truck again in the near future. Food trucks are ideal to promote your business due to their flexibility and ability to draw a crowd. In reality, having food trucks to the front of any establishment can immediately increase foot traffic to the vicinity of businesses.

The absence of the required ingredients

If you're fed up of purchasing fresh ingredients but not making money then this is the ideal option for you. Due to its ease of use and ease of use, customers may be tempted to take a bite at your restaurant. Food trucks are able to serve in any place and doesn't require lots of ingredients to be prepared unlike restaurants that require many ingredients to run their day-to-day business operations.

Small-scale Investment

If you're considering opening an operation for a food truck you'll be amazed at how affordable it is. Food truck businesses could begin at a cost of just $20,000 to $30,000. It can increase in size even without a huge capital investment. Also, this type of business requires less effort with regards to employees than the majority of restaurants.

A greater profit margin than eating establishments that cook in-house

This could be one of the reasons to incorporate an attempt to incorporate a food truck into your company. According to recent research that show sales volume and revenues per truck is around 20% higher than restaurants. The reason behind this is that food trucks already have a loyal customer baseand lots of people already make regular visits to them.

High-Profit Margin Sales of Savory Snacks

Food trucks selling snacks that are savory typically earn greater profits than sweets like cakes or cookies since they need less effort and a simple method of preparation. In the case of catering to hungry customers who are hungry, you must concentrate on selling snacks that provide quick satisfaction, or people who prefer a relaxed lunch, like hot dogs, sandwiches, burgers and more.

A great source of income during the Initial 3 Months

According to a lot of food truck owners, the initial 3 months of operation are typically highly profitable, provided they have a good reputation within the local community. Food truck owners have significant turnover , and a lot of clients visit them frequently. This is one of the main reasons that people recommend to consider food trucks as a business.

There is no need to worry about Building Permits, permits, or opening an Account with a Bank

Like food trucks, food trucks don't require permit or construction permits as they're usually operating for short periods of period of time. This is particularly helpful when you need to move locations quickly without having to deal with the paperwork.

High-Profit Margin Even at Low Prices

Food trucks are sold at more than restaurants offering the same menu, because people appreciate variety and flavor.

Flavors and Freshness

If you want to offer an original menu and create a name for your company food trucks provide you with creativity, particularly when it comes to unique menu items and flavors. Also, you can utilize fresh ingredients to enhance your food with regard to flavor and appearance.

In addition to catering and restaurant business, Food Trucks Are Also Offering Their Products at events and pop-ups

Pop-ups are a great opportunity to experiment with your ideas, try your food , and evaluate your business. It's an affordable method to get your food in the market without having it confined to a particular location. Pop-ups are also excellent for testing the market. If you're attending retail shows or an occasion that's associated with an exhibition, it can be a great opportunity to exhibit your items. There you have the reasons to start a food truck.

Food Trucks Food Truck vs. Restaurant

Which of them is more sustainable or environmentally friendly to run? Or do we have a definitive answer? In the present, a lot of people are quick to admit the fact that trucks for food are the most unfortunate of the two negative effects of the nation's attention on how economically-sound techniques are tied to transportation techniques.

But sustainability is an essential element at any moment a light turns on; plastic gets tossed in the trash and dishes are cleaned, and so on. Green (or damaging) practices don't just begin and end with the turn of the ignition key but they do happen throughout and after each working day of a company, whether in the form of a food trailer, or in the usual physical cafe.

Look over the parts that may be the most significant elements during these tasks in business.

The Location

As you're likely aware caterers are on the move. They are mobile and leave a less impression of the place they've been. There's a small framework in addition to the kitchen for business which needs to be maintained. Then, there are restaurants. Cafés are a huge space that need to be lit regularly, cleaned, and control the temperature. The physical elements are constantly in existence and not just during work hours.

Energy Use

As mentioned above the physical space requires natural gas and electricity in order to maintain a comfortable temperature and provide light to dining patrons. In dining areas, the cooking process is typically performed using natural gas, as well as stoves and frying pans are heated throughout working hours. According to the results of 2003's Commercial Building Energy

Consumption Survey the majority of restaurants use 38.4kWh of energy per square foot per year, or roughly 77,000 kWh per year for the 2000 square. ft. eatery.

Food trucks also require a source of heat to cooking, and so they typically make use of propane. A year-round normal food trailer would use about 900 gallons propane, aside from the requirements for fuel for moving around. While this fuel is typically gasoline or diesel catering vehicles may also make use of biodiesel or vegetable oil. Additionally the onboard generator, onboard generators address the issue of electricity. Generators tend to be more polluting than grid power, food trailers require less power and are more dependent on sunlight.

Miles per Vehicle

Though restaurants don't have the capacity to add miles to their customers but their patrons are likely to travel to the usual eating establishments. A brief excursion with food trucks can often help offset other small outings by customers who have typically taken a drive to eat at an establishment.

Waste

The issue of waste is a major issue in the industry of food is an issue that runs through restaurants and food trucks. While certain catering trucks are green by using bagsasse made of corn, plastics made from corn, or repurposed take-out containers made of paper however they're creating trash. In contrast, restaurants can utilize dishes, cups and other utensils. Takeout and fast-food restaurants often rely heavily on take-out containers constructed out of Styrofoam as well as plastic.

Is there a winner yet? In this in-depth analysis it is clear that mobile food stands typically have less harmful environmental effects. It is entirely possible that some restaurants can be more eco-friendly in comparison to other trailers for food.

Remember, as a proprietor of a food truck be attentive to the needs of your customers. Your commitment to eco-friendly methods will attract a steady stream of customers and draw new customers to your company.

Chapter 2: Different Types

A food truck isn't your only method for selling food. There are other options and you should look them over before deciding to go all-in on the idea of a food truck. Certain options may work better for you.

Food Carts

You've probably encountered one. In the US they're typically connected with hot dogs and sandwich shop. It's easy to believe that's all they're great for but they're whatever you want to make them. In developing countries where food trucks aren't so common food carts can sell whole meals.

A few examples of meals that are sold are street food items which can be cooked quickly in the wok, soup and Ramen bowls. They are very popular in the US therefore it's not so much a problem to have one to attract the attention of. A typical food card is made from stainless steel and aluminum. They're flexible and can be utilized in a variety of ways.

The fact that they are portable allows you to set them up wherever and are more straightforward to obtain permits for. City officials do not have any car-related issues as opposed to food trucks and their mobility means that more locations are open to them. Instead of parking in an established spot and putting your cart directly up to officesand be sure to draw a steady stream of people.

The drawback is that you can't conduct so much business like food trucks will. Carts are less crowded and can only carry the amount of food you can take on. But, you can follow the same strategy that food cart sellers employ and get another to continue bringing you new items. You can store your food items in a designated location in a car or in your residence.

Repurposing an old food cart is also a simple process. If you attempt to offer only breakfast and discover that there isn't any demand and you want to serve lunch in later afternoons, all you need to do is remove several panels, and you'll be able to create a lunch-time cart. About 3 p.m. You can offer a snack cart in the afternoon serving coffee. This feature isn't available in food trucks. It's likely to appear strange when you see food trucks that serve pancakes throughout the day, Vietnamese cuisine for lunch or donuts and coffee in the late afternoon.

However, your chances to create brand recognition are slim and it's likely be difficult to grow directly from a food truck to a larger business. The goal is to save enough money for an automobile and then build from there.

Concession Stands

Fixed restaurants offer great meals and are low-cost. They also make sure that the owners earn profits. Concession stands are typically connected to movie theaters, however, the most lucrative are found in stadiums. These days, stadiums are laid with the capacity to serve diverse functions. Although multiple sports don't play in the same stadium concert and conference events frequently take place within them.

This is why hiring a concession stand at these times an excellent option. It's an event-related enterprise which means it's unlikely that you're able to count on them year-round. If you're looking to make some extra money or to explore the possibilities in the market, this is an excellent opportunity to test your ideas. Concession stands typically sell unhealthy food items, and as people become more conscious about their health there's a greater demand for healthier food.

You could offer healthy varieties of local cuisine to attract customers to your stand. While ethnic cuisine may not be the most popular option because of the short-term nature of these stands but it's something worth considering.

Kiosks and Booths

Food vending outlets are either permanent or mobile. Some locations have permanent spaces that are devoted to kiosks. Street fairs usually draw many people who visit food stands and kiosks. There are many kiosks appearing near beaches as well as in other areas of leisure.

They're not really portable, however at same the same time, a food booth isn't an enduring structure either. They're usually constructed and you can add your logo to them. Contrary to food carts that you cannot swap your branding. A food stand, or food kiosk can be described as a truck for food that doesn't have wheels. They are equally appealing however they lack the mobility of trucks.

The promise of a fantastic place replaces the absence of mobility. The city usually leases these to operators, and these locations are always home to an event or festival happening that draws visitors to the area. If the idea of driving around or buying vehicles isn't your thing then this is an excellent alternative.

Gourmet Trucks

Food trucks are generally believed to offer inexpensive and tasty food, however there is increasing numbers of food trucks that are gourmet. They sell meals that are priced more expensive than restaurants and have loyal fan bases. They are often used by chefs who want to start their careers.

Food trucks are a great way to showcase your talents on social media, which can help explain the rise in popularity of gourmet food trucks. Influencers are eager to evaluate the trucks and consequently If you're a budding chef or an entrepreneur, you'll be rewarded with amazing reviews. There's an increase of food truck rallies , where various food truck owners gather at one site, and people flock to these events. Food samples from various trucks is appealing to people, which in turn can increase the revenue that food trucks earn.

Restaurants and Bustaurants

It's an unofficial food truck. Why should you stick with food trucks when you can purchase an entire bus and place your customers in it? They're extremely well-known in Europe where people take public transport more frequently and are aware of the benefits of turning buses into restaurants. In London the old double-decker buses are transformed into cool eateries offering a distinctive dining experience.

Although the costs are more expensive, this is an opportunity that could be exploited within the US. People are bound to be drawn to a large red bus serving food because they've never experienced this before. You'll have to endure some of the first hurdles in obtaining permit requirements, yet it may prove worthwhile. The ability to place passengers in your bus and to run a takeaway business in the form of a food truck generally provides two options to attract clients. You'll require wait staff however, due to the small seating space there's no need to worry about the hassles of a fully-fledged restaurant.

Chapter 3: The Importance Of Having A Plan Is The Most Important Thing

Business Plan

Once you and your partner have decided which roles to take on and the best way to divide profit, then the first task to complete is drafting your business's plan. This is in which the main idea takes shape. We'll review some of the most important aspects that you'll need in your business plan. After that we'll take a look at an example of a business plan. First what is the reason you require one?

Business plans are essential for those seeking the capital of a third party, such as banks small-business administrations, or any other lenders.

Even if you're not required to create a plan for funding, the beginning preparation and organization are crucial in the overall success of the company and can assist you in avoiding costly errors.

In the event that partners are involved in developing the plan for business. In this case it's even crucial to ensure coherence of vision. This is crucial to avoid disputes that could endanger the survival of the company.

Take a look at some items that are unique to the food truck industry which should be considered in your plans.

It's the Local Food Truck Marketplace

The section on market analysis within the company plan among of the most difficult to write because it requires a large amount of data that is objective and gathered from the analysis of both the primary as well as secondary sources.

In this instance we're interested in starting the food truck industry. A little research into the industry and some statistics could be required, however the best research will be able to familiarize you with local brand names. This includes online research on the types of food trucks that are available in your region (to aid in branding and differentiation).

It is also sensible to search for "food truck parks." There are many cities that have parking areas that are leased out for use by group of trucks catering to the lunch-time business crowd. Many times food trucks are parked at these locations for the duration of their stay and have an underlying predictability that many food truck enterprises do not have. This could be the most secure spot to launch your business since there is a record of pedestrian traffic, reliable food costs, and regular sales, which are not common in the food truck industry. There is a risk that your company's brand needs to stand out from the offerings offered by other trucks.

It's also sensible to look up the local festivals, fairs and other events that are within 50 miles from your base. The information you need is easy to locate online and the organizers are usually willing to provide information on the cost for exhibits and attendance since they'd like you to attend. This can assist you to calculate costs and demonstrate to potential investors in which areas you plan to generate revenue for your business. After you've explored markets in your area, you'll be required to determine which trucks are that are in direct or indirect competition with the one you've imagined. Direct completion could be the menu that's which is substantially the same as the one you've imagined in your mind. You should ensure that you don't set your self up for competition against an established brand within a narrow market. There could be indirect competition, such as an similarity in menu. There is still enough variation in the menu that customers could likely be drawn to the two businesses separately, should they be in the same place. Modifying your menu could be an option to lessen the anxiety that comes from directly and indirectly competing.

Differentiation of the brand as well as the product offerings is crucial to the success of food trucks and should be an integral element of your business strategy. This doesn't mean that you can't launch a food truck just like other ones in the area however, it does mean that you should only do this after determining the strategy for competing with the truck. The method to be successful however, is usually more complicated than.

Do you provide better quality food, a wider menu, more hours of service or offer a more affordable price? Maybe some mix of the above?

Food Pricing

One of the toughest and most crucial aspects of creating a business plan is making the decision on pricing. For food trucks there are many methods and strategies to properly price your food items in order to attract your target customers and make an income. The price should be determined using the price of the raw materials utilized to prepare the food.

In general, restaurants will set their prices with a 35-45% markup of the cost of food which includes food plates, plates and garnishes. Let's suppose that you're serving a dish which contains ingredients that range from to $5. Then you could set the cost of $7.25. You can play around with pricing, and exclusivity could make costs rise. For example, stadiums for baseball typically offer $6 for a hot dog due to their exclusive access. Your lunch-time customers are more sensitive to the price than those attending a concert with the assumption that the prices are more expensive for food items. If you set your prices in a way that is too low, you will quickly realize your message to convey to customers is that your food isn't worth the price. Try it out, and you'll come up with a suitable price range for each item on the menu. If you're surrounded by other trucks, make sure to wander around the site to get a feel for their menus and costs. You shouldn't be charging $4 for a water bottle in a market where everyone else is charging just $2.

Another factor to consider is the amount of labor costs, both during preparation as well as at the point of service on the truck. If one item is more labor-intensive than other items offered You can modify the price in order to reflect this. In the absence of this, it could cause a decline in earnings that could discourage you, which can sabotage the likelihood of success of your food truck company.

Utilization of Strategic Partnerships

Strategic partnerships must be considered when preparing a business's strategy. The most popular lobster roll brand is based on the family's fishing connection to offer low-cost products which can be sold with a significant margin. The above is an illustration of a strategic partnership which can give an edge in the market which makes the business attracted to financing and increasing the likelihood of the business's success. Another example of strategic partnership could include lease rates that are favorable or exclusive deals offered by the owner of a company or festival organizers who take a tiny portion of the profits. It's worthwhile to think about who you know and how you can leverage these relationships to gain an advantage.

Also, even if don't have a connection with a supplier You should invest a lot of time interviewing and savoring food products for price negotiations, guarantee the quality of their products and to make sure your expenses are at a minimum. Your efforts to do this must be documented in your business plan so that you can present it to anyone who might invest in the growth of your company. When you are more established and are involved in diverse events, it's important to maintain your contacts with the those who organized previous events that you attended. There are many who are in the business, and they will provide you with notice in advance and provide great opportunities for great venues and events. It's also beneficial to partner with people who are part of the media. It doesn't matter if you support an organization that is recognized by the media, or provide an unusual food item that has been featured in the news and gets attention from the media, this will make your business a success. A lot of food trucks provide challenges with food, such as an 8-pound burrito which is available for free if two people are able to complete the food in less than one hour. It's not a lot of exposure from a cost perspective but a fascinating story and news outlets often like these opportunities to bring human interest with the news on slow days.

The planning for Food Quantities

When you are pricing your drinks and food be sure to consider acceptable and reasonable serving sizes. It is your choice to provide large portions in order to increase price or to draw customers, but you must start with the standard portions for calculation. If you intend to serve 20 percent more items, you can increase the price to 2% as an instance. Food trucks may also provide alcohol-based beverages, such as beer or wine. Make sure you check the local regulations to ensure that all licenses required have been obtained. We have provided an image projection tool at the end of the book to help with the planning of quantity.

Sample Plan for Business Plan Template

If you're not experienced in creating an effective business plan, here's an example template you could use to run your own food truck:

The Executive Summary section should describe what you're seeking to achieve and provide a broad overview of your company's image, and the method you'll use to run your business. This is a summary of what your business about.

Goals: In this section, you should define your primary as well as secondary goals of your company. In this section, you should explain the goals you intend to accomplish in the long-term and short-term.

Vision and Mission The mission and vision section should state your business's mission and vision, as well as the values of your business to showcase to investors your business's approach. This could be a way to emphasize freshness, sustainability and/or donating to an organization or charity in your area.

Summary of the Company: This will discuss more details about the business. It will include the owners of the company and their share of profits as well as the initial expenses which are required by the company, the location for the commissary or kitchen and food truck location.

* Ownership

* Startup costs for overhead.

* Kitchen location

* Food truck places

Services and Products The Products and Services section of your business plan should include an elaborate outline of the menu you'll offer to your clients. It is also necessary to provide an exhaustive list of ingredients that you will be using for the food that you will serve on your menu. Include the cost of food and anticipated sales prices.

* Menu description

* Raw materials source

* Sales literature

Market Analysis Summary Market Analysis Summary involves studying and studying your market, so that you can be able to make the right decisions to stay in tune to the current market conditions and your chosen segment.

* Industry analysis

* Analysis of competition

• Market trend analysis

Business Strategy The part on business strategy will assist in forming your own strategy for your food truck industry so that you are able to identify your competitive advantage and important connections, how to present your company's image in the marketplace as well as what price to set for your products and sell them, and with whom you should partner with.

* Competitive edge

* Brand positioning

* Pricing strategy

* Strategic partnerships

Marketing Strategy Marketing Strategy encompass the various media options that are able to help promote the product more. The two kinds of marketing that can be employed are traditional media for marketing, such as print or television as well as the digital marketing channels including internet-related and social media.

• Marketing media that are traditional

* Digital Marketing Media

management summary: This summary of management will summarize the people who are involved in the management department of your company. The organization structure serves to display who's in charge of what and what is the corporate structure. The section also looks at the types of employees and open positions. This is essential for the management to know who is likely to be employed for each position.

* Management team

* Organizational structure

* Staff to be hired

Financial Plan This section will look through the numbers of the company, including the finances and the figures. The first section will cover how to reach the break-even point for your business when you're just starting up. This is the sum of your costs and the potential revenue you might earn during the duration of the year. This is shown within the profits forecast alongside the other costs and break-even analysis.

* Break-even analysis

* Profit forecast

An important note about getting financing If your credit score is mediocre to bad you will need cosigner, as well as a substantial money down (as as a percentage of the total cost) or to offer a collateral that is viable like a house or vehicle; make sure that you know the potential risks. The better your credit higher, the lower your lender's expectations regarding cosigners, down payments and collateral. If you are able, try other lenders for the best conditions. A solid business plan could have a major impact on the answers you get by the lender.

The Right Mental State

If you wish to stand a an opportunity to be successful and success, you must start your process of developing your idea by eliminating things that are boring, like basic hot tacos, sandwiches and hot dogs or anything else that people can make at home and with similar quality. There was times when a food truck was able to thrive solely by giving its customers the convenience of. It was a method to walk from their offices and grab a quick snack to keep them going until 5 p.m. These days are long gone. In order to be successful in the current market, food trucks need to "wow" their clients. The new gourmet food truck market still provides convenience, but also delicious dining experiences. Few people are likely to be thrilled about paying a few dollars less for bland food. In today's food truck marketplace there is a rule of thumb: be extravagant or leave.

It doesn't need to be expensive or exotic It just has to be different and delicious. The "different" feature will help to boost your word-of mouth marketing channels. "Delicious," of course will leave your clients with a positive memories of something they'd like to revisit.

A lot of food truck owners choose to base their business on food from popular nations like Italian, Japanese or Mexican food. Some believe they should focus in a specific area that they are able to cook such as doughnuts or burgers. The best way to approach this is to know what your customers want and be able serve the market with the best available product. If you realize that your community's population is a fan of vegetarian tacos and you're the most well-known meat eater in the area, then consider launching vegetarian tacos. In the event that you launch a popular idea, it can give you the time that you need to make improvements or look for the ideal people to join your company.

Another approach to create an idea is to expand outwards from a specific type of food. Let's consider waffles as an instance. Your food truck might be known for waffles made using syrup, butter fruit toppings, gravy, fruit chicken, ham, and many more options from Sunday. Your customers are people who love waffles (almost everyone) and are also eager to try something new and interesting (again most people) This is what makes you stand out among every other "waffle establishment." From then from now, branding won't become difficult--"The Waffle Truck" first of all, written in large, prominent words will draw people in enough to take a look at your menu. Once they've seen your menu that is creative you'll be sure to find something they'll want to test. Sold!

In line with your personality and personal preferences, you might be better off sticking to an idea that you already know (if you're not a chef or cook, at the very least as an eater) and you're enthusiastic about. If, for instance, you're awestruck by authentic German Bratwursts which is why you'll be likely to ensure that your patrons always get the exquisite version of Bratwurst you believe is meant to be enjoyed. Your enthusiasm and enthusiasm will radiate, spreading to your employees and customers. However If your primary goal is to earn money, then you should try to find the most lucrative idea to fill a gap within your market.

Do a few walks through the market where you plan to put the food van. The term "marketplace" refers to any place where food trucks are operating for example, an open-air market or town square. Are there any particular foods kind that's not available? Perhaps an idea that's successful in a similar industry? There aren't any law or regulation that state you shouldn't operate the shawarma food truck feet from another food truck serving shawarma Be aware that you could be dividing the potential business. In addition, you'll encounter a more challenging local work environment. Not only will your competition be displeased with your move to the area as well, but also the city's officials and consumer bodies might not be happy with the addition of a food truck that does not contribute to the variety of the market.

A further important element to your idea may be with costumes. A lot of top Food truck companies have managed to stand out with their imaginative costumes, regardless of regardless of whether they're ethnically-based or unique in a different way.

Chapter 4: Finding The Right Medium

Your vehicle is your point of business and holds the crucial for your business's success. You'll have to choose the ideal truck, make sure that it's in your price range, and adapt it to your requirements. You may purchase the most attractive truck but if it's not able to meet your needs for cooking and requirements, it's not of any benefit. It's possible to spend lots of money, and adds to the cost of starting.

It's all about the money you spend to purchase your vehicle. In short, your car is a great way to eat up the largest amount of your initial capital. Making the right choice is crucial. Before even thinking about purchasing a truck visit your local county's office or city's office to meet with the person responsible for review of food truck design safety. Ask them to send you a brochure that contains all the rules and safety guidelines. There's no need to follow them right now however, once you've purchased your vehicle, you'll have to make it your own and these rules can save you from many difficulties.

Buying an SUV

It is possible to spend between $50,000 and $150,000 for a food truck. The price range includes new and used trucks of every size. It's tempting to cut expenses and choose the cheapest truck you locate. It's not always the best choice. Your truck is the place you'll conduct your business, therefore you'll need to consider the cost of maintenance and the functionality. The most important thing you'd like to avoid is for your vehicle to malfunction or require a lot of repairs.

New trucks are among the most reliable, and they come with the "shine" factor that is a plus for them. They'll also decrease in value like a rock dropped into the water. Depreciation means a reduction in value. Although they may be mobile restaurants, they're vehicles that are subject to wear and wear and tear. As with other vehicles, they're not utilized by anyone. Food truck owners who own other food trucks are the only ones interested in these vehicles. Depreciation will take an enormous hit.

On the other hand it is possible to keep the truck for a lengthy period of time if your company is doing well. The longer you hold onto it and the longer you can keep it, the less you have to be worried about depreciation. This is because even a used vehicle will appreciate to zero on an extended enough timeframe. If you've never had the opportunity to run previously then it's best to go to purchase a used truck. There are numerous challenges that you'll have to face, and it's ideal to reduce your expenses. If you've had a successful previous business, be it within the industry of food or otherwise, it's time to look into buying a brand new truck. You'll get a better understanding of the way cash flows function which is why it's worth the risk.

If you're a new business owner, you might want to consider hiring trucks. It's not the ideal option for financial planning but it will reduce the initial costs significantly. It puts the burden of cash flow on your company and you'll have to consider an additional expense. The decision of renting or buying comes down to. If you purchase a truck with a loan and you pay interest on a monthly basis, you'll be paying payment. What do these interest payments compare to the rental cost? Pick the less expensive option.

If you're purchasing a truck in cash (without the need for a loan) the decision is somewhat more complicated. Where would you have put the cash, and what cash flow would this investment generate? Let's suppose you decide to spend $2,000 per month for a rental truck and then invest the $80,000 that it would cost to purchase that truck in marketing. What happens if the excitement generated by the additional $80,000 contribute to at minimum $2,000 in monthly sales? If your typical purchase price is $10, that's 200 additional sales for the month, or seven more daily sales.

From a practical perspective an alternative to moving to a an area with a lot of traffic could generate an additional 7 sales each day. It's not a lot to achieve. In this instance it's better to consider purchasing the truck because it will get rid of the $2,000 monthly installment and change locations to make seven additional sales every day. Consider all your options before deciding which option to choose.

Your psychological state also plays an important part. Certain people feel better off renting home rather than purchasing them. This makes estimating cash flow much easier and is easy to change strategies. If your current selection of food doesn't work it's easy to hire a new truck and not have to modify the one you have.

Maybe a middle of the road solution would work best for first-time owners. You can rent a truck for first three months to gain an accurate view of cash flow. Purchase a new truck following that in line with how your company is performing. If the business is good, then buying the truck will increase your monthly cash flow and your company will be able to acquire assets.

Lowering Costs

Trailers are an excellent choice when you're in a pinch for money. They're less expensive than trucks and range from $15,000 to $50,000. A trailer is less expensive but there are additional expenses you'll need be aware of. In the beginning, you'll need to cover parking fees for the trailer as well as your car. The trailer is less mobile as you'll need to connect it to your vehicle in order to haul it all over the place. In addition, if you don't own the vehicle to haul a trailer, it's an additional cost. If that's the case, then you could be able to make the purchase of a food truck.

It's not as easy as it sounds however, it can be difficult to lease trailers. There are opportunities to find deals in classified ads or lease one from a different owner who has no immediate need for it. The deals aren't plentiful, so don't count on them. Trailers are also generally larger than food trucks meaning you'll need to make concessions. Do these compromises force you to serve fewer food items? It's important to take this into consideration.

The costs associated with beginning a business can be expensive It is important to think of the initial expenses as investment. It's unlikely that you'll receive your money back in one day, but you will make an asset that pays you over time. Many business owners who are new to the field consider their initial costs against their monthly earnings by using a breakeven calculation. For instance, if you put up $80,000 upfront and earn $1,000 every month, it's going to take eighteen months to make back the money.

This is an error in business decision. If you invest $80,000 you're creating a valuable asset that is able to be sold at some point in the future. If you are able to sell your old Food truck at $50,000 then your true investment is $30,000. (80,000-50,000.) If you pay $1,000 monthly, it will earn the money over 30 months. If you're making an average salary of $4,000 per month, the actual income from your business is $5,500 per month. Your time to recover has now been reduced to just six months.

Furthermore, if you're thinking to own the vehicle for a long period of time, will it matter the amount you pay for it in the beginning? If you have enough cash to fund the purchase, it's not a factor. It is important to concentrate on creating the best asset that you can. For instance, you could purchase an Ice cream truck for $150,000, however this could be an issue if you're serving Mexican food. A used truck worth $70,000 is more beneficial. However, if the $70,000 truck isn't providing sufficient space for cooking fantastic food and serve your customers the best food, it's not an ideal asset. A truck worth $90,000 could be more suitable.

If this truck is able to allow you to cook delicious food in a hurry, travel quickly and safely to your destinations and won't run the maintenance costs this is a great asset. It will yield more profit it compared to those who have a $70,000 car. You'll pay higher, however you'll earn more. Consider your purchase of a truck in this way. While I'm not saying that costly is more desirable, but far from it.

The value of your investment is determined by the asset you generate. Don't think about it as a matter of the amount it will cost you. Instead, consider how much money it will bring you and how quickly it is able to do it. Compare its cost to the amount of money you have and then make a wise choice. What if the truck you want to buy for $90,000 is ideal however, you're only able to afford the $70,000 model? You're likely to encounter this situation. If that occurs, you'll have several options.

Do you have the money to purchase a trailer equivalent to the truck with a price of $90,000? If you already have a towing vehicle, then a trailer is the ideal choice for you. If you don't own an automobile, and aren't able to negotiate a price for trucks with a price like $90,000 you can consider leasing a truck similar to it for a couple of months. You can keep the $70,000 or significant portion of it in a savings account with interest and add your monthly income to the account. As it grows to $90,000, purchase the vehicle. You can also save up until you are able to pay for a down payment on the $90,000 truck , and then purchase it with the loan.

Don't compromise and purchase an inferior product simply because it's less expensive. If a truck that costs $70,000 isn't generating money then you're certainly not "saving" the money. It's actually making you more money. A lot of first-time entrepreneurs fall into this trap. You must consider assets, not expenditures. Any expenditure that makes your business more profitable and generates money for you is a good investment in the event that you can manage it. If you aren't able to afford it, start saving until you are able to.

Picking an appropriate truck

How do you determine which one is the right fit for you? There are several aspects to consider before purchasing a truck. The most obvious one is the kind of food that you'll serve. Certain trucks are equipped with kitchen appliances, but others do not. If you're purchasing a secondhand vehicle with appliances, you shouldn't pay an extra price for them. Appliances that are used sell at a price that is lower than 10 percent of the cost of purchase. If the seller uses these to justify their price, don't go for it. You can purchase second-hand appliances and put them in place yourself.

The type of food you prefer will determine the amount of space you'll require. If you're making pizzas in the truck, you'll require additional space for an industrial oven as well as dough preparation. If you're grilling burgers you'll not require any space as an oven that is hot is plenty to meet your requirements. When you're serving up a variety of soups, such as those found in Asian cuisine, you'll require significantly less space. Think about how you would like your kitchen space to appear like and assess trucks in line with that.

The type of food that you'll prepare also determines if you'll use commercial kitchens to cook meals or. For instance, an Asian soup-based meal does not need much cooking on site. But, you'll need an area to cook the food in advance. If this is the type of food you prefer it is possible to choose a small trailer and then invest the majority of your funds into commercial kitchens. The requirement to have a kitchen for commercial use must be considered in conjunction with the vehicle's expenses. If you are able to get a larger truck that can cook all your meals in it and save money on the expenses which a commercial kitchen can produce.

However, the majority of food truck operators require an office space in order to produce tasty food. Again, it is important to consider assets, rather than going with the expense-based thinking process. This will directly impact the cost of your decisions like I mentioned previously. When choosing a truck it is important to look at the locations you are considering. A larger truck may not be able to maneuver smaller spaces.

In general that the bigger your vehicle is, the lesser the amount of places that work for it. A smaller vehicle can fit to more places, however, in the event that it's too small you'll be unable to cook any decent food within it. The balance is what you have to be striving at. Your customers' personalities also play into your decision to choose a truck. There are certain expectations that customers have about your company and, when they see it as visually unappealing, the food's flavor won't matter nearly to them as much. People will flock to you for great food if you're a good cook but it's more difficult to get them to come to you when your truck doesn't appear appealing or look like is supposed to.

If, for instance, you're serving pizzas out of a tiny truck the customers may think they're reheating frozen pizzas and the perception of your company's image decreases. The design of your truck is also crucial. Food truck owners often alter the look of their vehicles by adding accessories to stand out. Does your truck have the right features for this? If it's not capable of accommodating certain modifications to the design and features, then it's not an investment worth making.

How many people are you expecting daily as well as how many workers do you need? This will affect the space requirements. Food trucks that serve numerous customers will require additional room for storage of ingredients as well as other equipment that is that are relevant to the food you're making. The business will require at minimum one additional employee who cooks food.

The majority of food trucks need at least two employees to serve customers. One person is responsible for coordinating orders, pay customers and serve food. Another person will prepare food and monitor the quantity of ingredients. Another person could be needed to lure customers to a food truck and manage the lines. If lines are getting long, it's a great idea to keep the customers entertained by offering customers a drink and asking for the money before they place an order for food.

Locating Dealers

In dealing with trucks dealerships, you'll have to use all your negotiation skills. They are experts at sell to business owners, and their abilities are higher-end than the average used car salesperson. But, you can get good offers on trucks by contacting an dealer near your home.

One method of determining the most affordable truck prices is to contact current food truck operators and inquire about where they purchased their trucks. Ask them about the performance of their trucks and what they recommend to other customers. You'll learn some excellent tips on what to look out for when purchasing the truck. You never know, they may even offer to sell their vehicle to you.

Customization

The purchase of a truck is only the beginning. It is important to modify it to fit your needs and this can be a challenge. If you've completed the required steps you'll have a clear idea of the things you'll need. At a minimum you'll have your menu planned at this stage. Make a list of all the things you'll need to keep in your truck. What will your cooking method take on? What food items will you keep in the truck, what kinds will be cooked and what equipment will you require to cook the food? The list of food storage requirements and the methods for preparation in detail can be helpful in designing the process.

It will also assist you in choosing the best equipment. Also, make it a habit to include any future menu items you can imagine. This will make it easier to plan ahead and ensure that you don't encounter costly design changes later on down the line.

Check Your Equipment

Now is the time to get all the kitchen equipment you'll need to cook with in the kitchen. Prepare a thorough list with specifications. Food equipment is divided into three categories. They are food preparation storage, cooking. At a minimum all food trucks require a grill, or a kitchen area, refrigeration as well as warm plates to cook food (hot plates.) The requirements of your particular business will differ in the way you decide to manage your operations.

Be aware that you cannot take your stovetop from the kitchen and put it in the truck. Commercial food equipment must comply with safety standards. It's recommended to talk to the proprietor of a truck, or the truck vendor to learn about these requirements. If you're buying a brand new model from the manufacturer they'll handle all of your needs.

If you're using an older truck the equipment it comes with must already be in compliance with commercial standards. But, if you're planning to install your own equipment, you'll have to go over these guidelines once more. Take measurements of the cooking area in your kitchen, and take note of the doors, windows and service windows and electrical outlets. Photograph a lot of your kitchen and record the measurements. For trucks that are brand new it is recommended to draw an engineering sketch that is detailed and then present it for the manufacture.

You can sketch out an outline of the design you'd like and then engage a freelancer via sites like Fiverr as well as Upwork to design your concept's 3D and 2D rendering. Certain manufacturers have internal design and mock-up facilities which you can take advantage of. They'll charge you however, it's bundled in with the price of purchasing a brand new truck. Note down the flooring materials that are in use as well as the air vents.

They are crucial. The inside of your vehicle will be extremely hot and the most important thing you'll want is an ignitable surface near you. Take note of exhaust vents too. In the event of an older vehicle it is important to ensure that everything functions according to the specifications. If you're buying a vehicle from dealers, they'll generally give you the maintenance history as well as the condition report. If you purchase through an individual seller, it is recommended to employ an electrician and a mechanic. They can inspect whether the vehicle is in good condition. They can also check the state of the car as well as the condition of appliances.

Water and Power

Your appliance determines your power and water needs. It's not possible to plug your appliances to an outlet, which means you'll require the power source from outside such as generators. Also, you'll need to take into account propane tanks for storage of water, propane tanks as well as other storage systems for energy. An electrician can help you identify this issue and suggest the best installation for you. Do not attempt to tackle this aspect of your vehicle. The water and electrical systems should be in good working order to ensure that you run your business without hassle.

The most frequent maintenance issues stem from the plumbing and wiring inside your truck. The car itself is transported between various locations, which means it won't suffer as much wear and tear as a normal vehicle. There won't be numerous oil or engine problems. The kitchen is the one that needs regular maintenance. Therefore, ensure that everything inside it is working properly from the beginning. If your kitchen goes down, so does your business.

Exterior Things to Consider

Although the inside is about effectiveness, the exterior is about the way you can draw customers to your truck. What kind of accessory do you require to ensure that your customers are served and enjoy your vehicle? For instance, numerous trucks add an outside counter of the truck to store napkins and condiments. Customers are able to eat their food without disturbing the inside and outside of the vehicle.

There are other external options you must consider. For instance the security awning is an ideal choice. These awnings are able to slide onto the front of the vehicle and shield the windows, doors as well as anything else that you may have attached to the exterior of your vehicle. They'll help prevent vandalism or other harm that may be caused by leaving your vehicle unattended for the night.

A retractable awning provides your window for order an intimate feeling. It can be extended upwards to protect your customers. The benefit of this awning is the ability to hear your customers' orders more clearly because there is acoustic insulation in the space. The awnings also prove useful when it snows or rains. People will be more likely to choose the truck that has an awning when it rains or snows as opposed to one that doesn't.

External TV panels can appear too fancy However, they're actually easy to put up. Food trucks may prefer to attach chalkboards to the outside of the truck and use them to display menus. Each day, the owners draw menu items on the chalkboard with chalk. Moreover If you're an artist who can draw intricate designs with chalk is worth the effort. But, if you're just like most people, the only thing you'll have to do is get the dirt on your fingers.

A TV panel is able to display the menu items of your choice and can also include graphics. A LCD panel isn't anything these days, and they're completely programmed. Make sure that you have a backup system to display your menu should the electronics malfunction or begin raining. Some trucks wrap them in the body to shield the screen while other trucks simply attach a TV to outside. It will make more use of your vehicle however, they'll also draw people into the vehicle if they're attractive.

Speakers can also be helpful. They can play music or letting announcements be made through speakers creates a sense of community between your customers. It will surely keep them entertained as they wait in the line. Another accessory that can help customers feel relaxed is a misting device. This is particularly true in hot environments. Customers will appreciate it. It'll put stress for your system of water however, it's an investment worth the investment.

There will be windows for service It is a given. Size of the windows could be altered based on your requirements. Larger windows for service perform better over smaller windows. They also function as excellent vents. The benefit of big windows that allow ventilation is that your customers can be able to smell the food you're cooking, which can be an another reason to visit. Don't have your service window too large that it's difficult to maneuver. It should have clear signage that tell your customers where they can order their food and the location where they can collect their food items.

A large component the exterior of your business is the vinyl wrap. It is a part of your marketing strategy as well as. An exterior wrap can make to make you stand out more. So long as it doesn't interfere with other functions of your truck It's a great option.

Approving the Design

This is the difficult part. Your plans have to be converted to engineering plans that define the dimensions and dimensions of your kitchen's exterior and interior. Additionally, you'll need to draw blueprints to show the plumbing system and fire protection equipment. You can either hire an independent contractor to create these for your needs, or employ the services of an industrial manufacturer.

The designer will have the capability to design drawings as well as knowledge of the most current safety and health regulations. You won't have be concerned about the plan getting rejected. But, they are expensive and you'll need to purchase an entirely new truck. Check with current food truck owners to get recommendations for designers. Design-only companies will give you any technical specifications that you require however, it's hard to locate the right ones for first-time buyers.

When your drawings are completed After you've finished your designs, you'll have to have them examined by the local authority. Find your local county office to determine the official responsible for the review of food truck safety plans and make for an appointment. If all is well the design will be approved and you'll have to put it into practice. Be aware that even food trucks have to be approved approval regardless of whether they've been approved to use before or not.

If you require changes for your design, you'll need to change the design. It could take some time to make it perfect when you're working on it yourself. Therefore, be patient and be patient in doing it. Keep your safety and the health of yourself, your employees and customers in the forefront of your thoughts. This will help reduce the likelihood of negative future negative reviews.

The purchasing and designing process is a complex. It's easier if you choose to partner with a company with previous experience, however the downside is that you'll be paying more. If you choose to purchase a used vehicle, you'll need to work out a lot of things on your own, however you'll be paying less. It's your choice to determine what is the best option for you. Make sure to utilize your time in a wise manner and keep your budget limitations in your head always. You're trying to save money , but do not end up becoming penny-wise, but the pound foolish. Once your vehicle has been purchased and constructed, it's time to get into licensing and permits. licenses.

Chapter 5: The Topic Is Money.

Costs

Don't assume that you have to invest a few thousands on the business of a food truck and it's not a cheap way to run of a venture. It is important to consider several factors before you get to a point at which you are confident about the sum of money you're investing in that business since it's going to require several dollars to ensure the food truck is off to a good start.

What costs for a food truck company? That's an easy question to answer. One of the most intriguing aspects of the food truck industry is that a large portion of the expenses will be allocated for legal costs that are specifically related to getting permits that are appropriate as well as insurance and legal assistance. Additionally, certain legalities are time-bound in certain states or, in other words you must be waiting for a place on the waitlist prior to getting one. What do you think that specific legality is? This is the right thing to do: becoming a holder of your Mobile Food Vending Unit Permit in order to run your vehicle! There are other costs associated with making sure that potential employees are up to speed. A lot of food truck owners are able to lend a hand to ensure their operations run efficiently, so it's important to consider when you're considering running an extremely large food truck company. Let's now examine a cost breakdown for a typical food truck. These numbers, derived from a resource for food trucks are actually based on figures that are derived from the East Coast region of the United States, specifically (and obviously) New York City. If you're planning on launching an eatery in the East Coast, these figures can be a good estimate to consider as a starting point for estimating the cost. The figures are estimates. East Coast, the USA

* Truck $50,000 (covers the purchase cost and the basic retrofitting).

Food vending machine permit: $200 plus possible waiting-listing (may run $15,000, if acquiring by a third party).

* Monthly payment: $500. month; estimated to cost at minimum $6,000 annually.

General liability insurance, business: $3,500-4,000 annually.

* Mobile vendor license: $100 (accounts for approximately $50 to take classes and $50 for a two-year license).

* Insurance for trucks: $2,000 to 3,000 annually (estimates suggest $2,500 annually).

* Commercial kitchen: Approximately $2,000 to $5,000 per month (estimates suggest an average amount of $366,000 annually).

* The average wage for employees is $16 an hour (estimates differ throughout the year).)

* Workers' compensation: about $7000 per year (accounts for 3 employees can vary based on amount of workers).

* Accountant: 350 dollars each month (accounts for around $4,200 for the year)

A PR expert: Around $1500 for three month (accounts of at minimum $6,000 annually).

If you take the costs of all those and expenses, the total expense of running a food truck company amounts to around $150,000-200,000 which is just taking the cost of an average into consideration. However, food truck companies is rewarding enough to earn enough money to pay for those expenses.

Budget

The amount of capital required to start the food truck is contingent on the specific circumstances: Do you take out a loan? Do you plan to purchase a vehicle or trailer? Do you require a car for pulling the trailer? Does the food truck have a food truck installed?

Prices can be wildly different based on the city you're in and the season. Food truck owners usually sell towards the end of the peak season. There are many deals on the market, and less competition because customers aren't able make use of the food truck until the next season begins. Even if you don't plan to make use of your food truck immediately from the beginning, it's the perfect time to invest in it since you can negotiate affordable costs! Based on our experiences in WA the cost to begin the food truck range between $15,000 and $100,000. If you can find a great agreement and have the resources, it's very easy to have all the equipment you need for less than

$20,000. But, if you'd like the food truck of your choice delivered to your location it is possible to multiply the price by 5 at a minimum!

Find the funds to get Moving

To obtain the cash you require Here are a few options:

* Crowdfunding: There's a myriad of crowdfunding websites where you can showcase your venture and gain investors from around the globe. We're considering Kickstarter, Fund Me, Indiegogo and many others. The majority of these platforms will require a portion of the money you raise and operate for a short period of time. Your project must be consistent and engaging so that people are enticed to put their money into it. Additionally, you should provide rewards>> for donors to Kickstarter such as. PayPal recently announced its crowdfunding platform that is said to have no charges. Learn more about these platforms and choose the one that suits you best!

* Take out a loan: Another alternative is to take out an advance through your banking institution. You'll need to have a sound business plan that

you can present to your banker in order to get the loan approved. Unfortunately, it's very difficult to obtain loans in Australia for the purchase of food trucks. We've seen some requests for loans being denied for food trucks. Banks aren't able to recognize the fragility of the market and food truck's volatile nature.

* Family and friends You may also ask your friends or family members to help you invest in your food truck, if they're willing to contribute.

Finding the Best Way to Find an Food Truck

You can find the majority of food trucks or trailers available for auction on Gumtree which is the most popular marketplace. You can also make use of the Facebook marketplace that is expanding exponentially and you can also look into Facebook groups specifically for food truck owners.

If I buy an established business, is it the right choice for me?

Sometimes , owners sell their entire company through their truck for food, which essentially means everything: you will take over their recipes and their location, as well as their regular customers, and their social media. It's not like you begin from scratch and rely upon a company which is already established. This is typically more costly when compared with starting from scratch however, if you have the money and the numbers that they offer you are satisfactory and you're ready to jump into action! It could be beneficial in case you don't wish to handle all the administrative work and create your own food truck and decorate it and so on. In this instance the owner of the truck has already completed everything, and there's not much to do. If you're looking to create your own concept you should consider purchasing the blank> food truck. Of obviously this is a more lengthy process. You'll not be able to immediately enter the field and be required to put in a lot of effort to achieve it, but it's an extremely satisfying and inspiring experience to get your truck in place and to develop your own ideas! We were searching to find food-trucks, businesses available for sale had a minimum price of $50,000 but we could not be able to afford it. We also wanted our menu as well as our idea. A trailer for setting up was the ideal solution!

Buy a brand new or second-hand food truck

This, too, is contingent on your budget as well as what you intend to accomplish using your truck for food. In Australia the variation in cost between a brand new vehicle and one that is secondhand could be substantial.

Buy a new food truck: A new food truck can give you greater safety from an engineering perspective as well as the durability of the material. Be aware that value of new vehicles is significant as it loses much of its value when you've used it, and it will be difficult when you decide to sell it for the same price that you purchased it at. The depreciation rate is higher for the new food truck as when compared to an older one. We approached firms that specialize in creating custom food trucks. they gave us estimates that could be as high as 100,000 dollars!

* Purchase second-hand food trucks: purchasing a second-hand food truck is a lot of some work to

make it fit for the specific needs of your project (buying equipment that is compatible with the kind of food you'd like to provide) but it's much less to purchase. You may also be able to sell it faster! This is the option we decided to go with according to our budget and the project we were working on.

Costs of Equipment for an empty Food Truck

We purchased the trailer for food by an Indian restaurant owner who already had it for various events. It was already fully-equipped and met all security requirements. The fridge was already in place and a microwave, as well as several utensils and benches made of stainless steel. Electricity and plugs were in place too. This allowed us to save on equipment. But the inside was not very well-fitted out, and we were able to not modify it as we had envisioned.

If you decide to purchase an unfinished food truck you'll need to think about the amount of time and money needed for its construction. You'll need to set up everything necessary to be in compliance with the standards including an electric system for appliances as well as lighting as well as sinks and the plumbing system, a venting system for your roof and isolating material for walls, the flooring, appliances, etc.

We paid around $7000 over the trailer's cost to build it up and furnish it. We added a ventilation system to its roof. We also added an additional sink and crepe machine and a kitchen robot, an raclette machine, exterior painting and menus as well as a few kitchen utensils as well as storage containers.

Do you want to rent or purchase your own food Truck?

Instead of buying a food truck, it's often possible to lease one. This isn't a common practice as we've not seen anyone doing it, however this might be a good option if you are looking to try out the waters before committing to the business. We have met with a few owner who had their own catering trucks as well, and at the same time we're also renting the truck out. If you can only find advertisements for food trucks on auction, do not be afraid to reach out to the seller and ask whether he'd be interested in renting the truck. A few disadvantages could arise when you lease food trucks. If you are forced to cancel events due to the fact that the food truck isn't in operation or you need to be set up for two weeks prior to the owner, it can cause annoyance! The purchase of a food truck lets you remain flexible, and be able to do whatever it's what you want. We wanted to eat our food truck since we had a plan that we wanted to create our own. We contemplated renting it and making a sale (it took us a while to find a buyer who was serious). We decided to abandon the idea since it would have involved a lot of administrative steps (because the insurance as well as the trailer were registered under the name of our company). The decorations were already applied to the trailer that was used for food. It would have been difficult for anyone else to make it work for the specific requirements of their customers.

Chapter 6: Learn The Rules

Food truck operators are restricted, just like those in the industry of restaurants. The two main areas covered by the rules include truck construction as well as rules on sales. The regulations in your city must be understood because they affect all aspects of your company from start to finish.

In terms of the kind of food that you could offer to customers who wish to be within a metered parking spot in order to be able to sell your food. Laws will govern almost everything related to your food truck's operation. Make sure you are aware of laws that are most likely to affect your company (or employ someone who is knowledgeable about).

You must be aware of applicable local regulations and laws that pertain to sales of food trucks in your town before purchasing the step van you've been tracking on eBayTM. When deciding on the key aspects of your business local regulations play a crucial part. The regulations will impact how your truck will be built, how your company will operate, and the way your company will be staffed. Before proceeding with any other activity anyone who is aspiring food truck business owner must thoroughly examine local laws to make sure that your mobile company is compliant with your local municipal regulations and laws.

You must be as thorough as you can be when studying local laws. Don't just ask your suppliers for rules or go on the internet for a detailed description of the regulations. Study the regulations and learn the rules for yourself. To find out the specifics of local laws yourself, visit the health department in your area. If you are unsure you have questions, get them in writing.

Also, be sure to meet with the health department's representative who is in charge of mobile food, and the department that has the responsibility of determining appropriate sales locations for the municipality in question, whether it's parks transport, urban planning. Working in these divisions and with a decision-maker will help you when confronted with possible regulatory concerns or issues.

You need to be aware of and know the local laws as an entrepreneur in the food service industry that is mobile. You can print them out and keep them in your bag every day until you are able to comprehend the regulations.

Licenses

Licenses are legal documents issued by a government agency that grants you the authority to perform any activity or use any item. In certain instances, following an examination, a license is issued to make sure that the individual who receives the license is able of doing a specific task However, the business license generally does not require any inspection of any sort.

The kind of food can be served by a food truck is one of the ways in the way that food trucks are controlled. The most common distinction is between processing trucks that serve food prepared in the truck, for example tacos, burgers or waffles, and those that are not processing serving prepared off-site, packaged food items. Since production trucks cook food that are prone to food-borne illness, the main distinct feature is that they are a higher threat to the health of the public. Modern processing techniques mean that it is now possible to create trucks that are safe to sell processed food items. Local laws could keep pace with modern technology as time passes.

Vehicle License

In the first place, in order to have your truck running on streets, you'll require an automobile license. Along with your truck and driver, the person driving the vehicle must also be licensed as a driver. Certain states have a requirement for a commercial driver's licence to operate a truck in accordance with the size and the mass of your vehicle.

Business License

Once you have your vehicle on streets, get a business permit to begin selling your products. The business permit is your official identification of your company, which obliges you to work within your local market and in the jurisdiction you are operating. Local and federal governments are legally required for small businesses to obtain the required business license prior to offering products or services. This permits your business to be registered with the government to ensure that you're legally liable for taxes on the gross profits you earn.

License Tax

A EIN or employer identification number is likely to be required if operating a business. It may be your Social Security number, if you are sole owner. It could also be that you require franchise or sales permits that you must obtain to ensure compliance according to the state where you are working.

State Permits

Permits are a type of permit that a government agency issues. Permits typically provide protection, and are usually issued following an exam.

Each state might have its own permits for operations or health which are required to establish your business. For more information, we strongly recommend visiting the SBA permits and licenses website.

Local Permits

The town you live in might also require permits for signs, sanitation taxation, zoning, or alarms. For details, we suggest the above-mentioned links and the official website for the city in your region.

On streets that are public, some market vendors provide street vending. It is usually restricted in some way by times or locations. Most often, trucks are expected to offer similar products in a specific distance from other businesses. While street vending could allow you to access many sales outlets however, it can be a challenge as there is always competing for the best location. Some cities allow exclusive private areas for food carts or food trucks. Lots sales have proven to be extremely successful in markets for example, Portland as well as Austin. However, in the markets that street-vending is allowed, like New York City and Los Angeles lot sales have been a popular option.

Food Licence

Similar to how the health department demands that every restaurant to be examined Your mobile restaurant will also require an inspection from the local health department and approval to make sure that your food is safe and well-maintained.

Liquor License

If you want to sell alcohol in addition to food items on your truck, you'll need an liquor license. This license isn't simple to obtain since it is contingent on the state you'll operate your business.

Music License

You'll require an music license in order to play music with copyright rights if you intend to use music to attract your customers. It's contingent upon the laws of the state where you operate your business. If you do play music from your CDs you may need a license since you are not able to use someone else's copyrighted music to run your own business without obtaining an official permission from them.

Employer Requirements

It is essential to verify that they are legally able to operate within your area before you hire staff. Employers working in the United States must complete I-9s which prove eligibility for employment and W-4s to calculate income tax withholding. The IRS offers an IRS tax guide for employers on their site for more details. If you are an employer, then may even be required to display these posters to staff. If you want to discuss the benefits of employees, such as unemployment insurance and insurance coverage for auto/general liability for your business You should get in touch with an insurance professional who is qualified.

Effectively avoid government Red Tape

Here's how to stay clear of bureaucratic red tape in the government:

1. Make an appointment with the appropriate Environmental Health Department.

2. Request a peddler's permit.

3. You can apply for an insurance policy for civil liability.

4. Buy business licenses and permits.

5. Get a kitchen or a storefront (depending on the kind of services).

6. Purchase high-quality, custom-designed food truck mobile trucks and trailers, in addition to other equipment that is required, such as storage containers, generators coolers, etc.

7. Utilize a checking account for business to make financial transactions.

8. Make sure you hire the workers of the food truck.

9. Get permits and licenses for businesses from local authorities like Health, Fire, Police and more.

10. Bank accounts that are open for credit card and cash transactions.

11. Learn about the equipment that is used to run the truck food industry.

12. Get the necessary safety training concerns for customers and employees.

13. Director and the leadership for the Food Truck company.

14. Develop a training plan for employees.

15. Purchase supplies, inventory, and ingredients.

16. Develop relationships with wholesalers as well as suppliers.

17. Select a menu option that is most appropriate for your food truck's needs.

18. Purchase or modify food truck trailers and mobile trucks in accordance with the kind of service that will be offered, and the style of your food truck's operation.

19. Get the necessary permits through local health departments, such as Sanitation License food Permit or Certificate and Health Certificate, etc.

Chapter 7: Team

managing staff may be the most challenging task of managing staff of all. It is essential to hire those with culinary expertise and are trained in the most safe food handling practices and are able to communicate with colleagues. You'll be hiring employees from different backgrounds, so you need to be capable of managing the employees. Effective communication is essential to ensure that your company operates efficiently, and you will require personnel who are adept at managing multiple tasks and communicating their progress all day long.

The food service industry that is mobile rarely needs culinary expertise for jobs in the kitchen and back of house. It is however advisable to seek out people who have worked in catering, restaurants or cooking schools since they already have experience of food production and security. The most important thing is that they be able to show all their certificates for health and hygiene and be current on their tetanus vaccinations.

The employees will be able to demand decent salaries. The initial salary for kitchen employees is about $12 an hour. It will typically rise after a few years when they are at the upper end of the salary scale. If you are hiring staff part-time and provide them with incentives, such as free food or food vouchers. This is especially true when you own an eatery or catering company.

The primary responsibility of everyone on staff is to manage garbage disposal. Each shift should be provided with their trash bags to prevent mixing food items with other garbage. It is also necessary to equip them with gloves and aprons.

Employ non-food serving staff

They will also accept orders, take payments and assist customers. They will also be accountable to clean their trucks following the departure of customers. They can also be offered complimentary meals to attract the best employees. You could even create a the system of tipping them when your clients are generous.

Food safety is among your main concerns, therefore you must ensure that everyone who handles food is clean and is free of illnesses. It is important to be extra careful about this since customers could be able to complain about the hygiene and health of your employees.

While interviewing, you must be on the lookout for candidates who appear uninterested in the work or lack confidence. In addition to responding to your questions and giving you references, you need to ensure that they are active and enthusiastic. If you find that a candidate isn't positive, don't take them on! They can affect the enthusiasm level of your employees.

Your counter will be paid staff approximately $10 an hour. However, you shouldn't expect customers to tip you as your main source of revenue. Some people do tip after they're extremely pleased with their experience, however the majority of them will not.

Make Your Staff Train!

Employees must go through training prior to their first day of work for your company. Conduct an in-depth interview and ensure that all employees know their roles within the company. They must know what they have to accomplish in any situation.

Make sure that you offer regular training for all your employees. The aim of the training is not just to teach them how to do their job but also to create a sense of bonds and instill the feeling of being motivated. This will help them become group members, and to feel that they're serving more than just for a paycheck.

As an chef, you be required to create your menu and supply your employees with the necessary information about the food items to prepare them correctly. You might also have to purchase the equipment needed to prepare the meals.

Chapter 8: Marketing

Marketing is all about knowing your customer's preferences and what they would like to purchase. It is possible that you have a plan to run a food cart but prior to launching or decide on your menu, you should meet with potential customers and take tests, test, try! These initial tests can help confirm the validity of your concept and menu, theme ingredients, attitude and much more!

If your strategy for marketing is not working No amount of public relations or advertising can help. There are many methods to promote a product or service. Many businesses employ the same methods of marketing, while some are more creative in creating a marketing strategy.

In the modern business world marketing can take on incredibly innovative styles. There are a myriad of options to use tools and a myriad of channels to promote our business. Marketing could be as simple as a printed flyer that is copied and distributed directly to individuals as well as far more complex with extensive preparation and complex productions. There aren't any strict rules for marketing. Innovation and research are usually the most important elements in an effective marketing strategy.

Many of us have inventive ideas on how to convey messages to potential and current customers. Some individuals naturally think of concepts that can help in promoting businesses. However, some of us struggle with marketing, and this is when you have to consider whether you'll assign the job to somebody else. Consult your partners or colleagues for suggestions. You never know! There's a chance that you have a marketing genius working in your company! In certain situations you might need to engage a specialist in marketing to design a successful marketing strategy for your business. It's true that this is an expense for your food truck company but the extra expense could be worth it over the long term.

There are many aspects of the marketing of a food truck and they all function together to boost the growth of your business. Certain strategies are long-term and others are tiny promotions planned around specific occasions and holidays. The majority of this will be on social media. However, some are more tangible on a daily basis.

Facebook

Facebook can be an effective marketing tool that can increase the number of customers you have when you are able to make use of it effectively. Facebook has a huge reach when you have the right users. The statistics of Facebook users are astounding and continues to amaze researchers. The number of users on Facebook is staggering. 1.3 billion people active in Facebook and 680 million of them using mobile devices. The 18-34 age group is very active as 48 percent visiting Facebook when they get up and clocking around an average time of just 18 mins for each session! This means that if your food truck does not already have a Facebook account of your own food trucks, it's time to get one up and running now!

How to Increase Engagement

One thing one way to boost the engagement of your followers is to update your regularly. The frequency of your post will depend on your schedule, however I recommend 5-7 posts every week is an ideal amount to let your customers know that you're actively engaged with your Facebook page. An account on Facebook that is believed as active and being active with your fans is more likely to attract engaged followers who actually be attentive to your posts.

One way to easily post updates on Facebook is to share fascinating photos and videos of the most exciting day of business. They are more effective than content-based posts since people love to look through their timelines and posts that contain photos or videos typically get more interest. The more attention you get, your more likes could be able to receive.

If you publish an image post at first you may get one likes out of it. This can happen to all of your posts with images. It is possible that you do not receive any comments on your post and become frustrated by this process. This is a common reason for people to refrain from attempting to create an audience on Facebook. However, if you let those fears go and continue to update frequently, you'll eventually stumble across that one post that gets the momentum.

However, the level of popularity will vary in proportion to the quality of the content you're sharing with your followers. It is important to know the kind of information your followers are looking for about your company. Experts advise that followers need posts that are simple and quick to read since it is true that everyone is busy and the majority of people read headlines for information. Not only must your content to be short however, they must also to possess certain characteristics to draw them in, such as educating people about you or your product, engaging the audience in some way, or even inspiring your readers. Let me go over these three points in more specific terms in relation to Food truck advertising.

Educational Posts: As the title implies this kind of content is meant to teach your audience something that is beneficial to them. It could be your unique method of cooking French fries until they reach the ideal crispness or the ideal method of marinating meat to get the best flavor. You possess skills that other are eager to learn.

Entertaining posts: These types of posts can cover everything. But one of the primary factors is the ability to draw and hold the attention of readers. It can be a humorous or humorous posts. If you're having a particularly busy day, you could make a video showing how chaotic your kitchen could be, especially when there seems to be no end to the customers queue outside.

You may want to put several GoPro cameras both inside and outside your truck to catch any interesting events. The footage needs to be edited before posting however it's a great method to keep a camera in the area without affecting the cooking process.

In the industry of food trucks it is possible to include some of these ideas into your advertisements:

* Food images

* Ingredient images

Food truck images

* Photos of the team in the kitchen

* Your location or the venue

* Photos of guests who were special

* Special events that you are taking part in

* Photos of your truck at landmarks that are unique

* Close-ups on food items taken from inside your truck

* Equipment for cooking

Special menus on the daily.

* Signature dishes

"Backstage" pictures

* Impromptu photos during a service

* Photos of products that are new or menu items

* Ingredient shopping trips

* Mechanical problems

Email Marketing

Since the beginning successful marketers have utilized email to advertise their companies, products events, products, and more! Email marketing is an efficient way to send the message straight to clients. But, there were some who abused this tactic in the past and, as a result it was that the word Spam was coined. Despite the negative repercussions email marketing remains an effective and cost-effective method to get in touch with clients.

If I say cost-effective, you'll have to remember that email marketing tools aren't free, as Twitter as well as Facebook. However, it provides opportunities that Facebook and Twitter tools for social networking do not provide. You may ask, "Why should I spend money for marketing by email when I could utilize Twitter as well as Facebook for no cost?"

Website

A website can be an important part of your marketing strategy. If you don't have a site nowadays you're missing out on the possibility to let your clients know more about you 24/7.

Businesses can afford to spend a substantial portion of their budget for starting on web designers. If you haven't yet hired an artist to design your website I suggest you design it by yourself!

That's right! Make it by yourself! Do not worry if your do not have any programming skills. It's simpler than you might A lot of people who aren't technically adept have started their websites using WordPress. WordPress is an open-source content management system that has revolutionized how websites are constructed and maintained. The initial purpose was to facilitate blogging, but WordPress has developed to become the default management platform for a significant proportion of websites found that are online currently. It is no cost on all hosting plans that provide it.

The Pinterest board for Food Trucks

In the beginning of 2012, there was a stated 5 million active users using Pinterest with more than 1.5 million visitors per day. These users spent at the most 15 minutes per day using the site. Another amazing statistic is the fact that Pinterest generated more visitors on websites than LinkedIn, Google+, YouTube and Reddit all together!

Some businesses may struggle to find an affiliation with Pinterest in the event that there aren't many visual elements associated with their company. Food trucks could certainly benefit from this popular social network.

Before you begin pinning images, consider the names of the various "Boards" that you would like your images to appear on. A board is essentially a category or folder in which you arrange your photos. People on Pinterest can join any of your boards or all of them. In the case of Cheez Philly I can make one of the boards below:

* Cheez Philly

* Food Truck graphics

* Street Food

* Cheesesteak

* Gourmet Sandwiches

* San Diego Food Truck

* Yum!

You don't need to design all of your boards in one go however, you should come up with imaginative names that attract the attention of. When you pin a photograph you are able to add the description. Be specific when you write your message.

YouTube Marketing

Video streaming has become an integral element of how the world collects information and is a great way to entertain. One of the biggest and most popular video-sharing websites is YouTube which has the capacity of 300 minutes worth of content that uploaded every minute. YouTube has made the sharing of videos to the masses by hosting user-generated videos at no cost.

YouTube is not just an effective tool for business marketing If used correctly you can also create confidence and credibility for your business. It may appear as if it's not but YouTube is actually an extensive and sophisticated social media platform. Because of the simple nature of the

YouTube interface the videos uploaded can be distributed to other social media sharing platforms, such as Facebook, Twitter, your blog, website, or even via email communications. YouTube videos are able to quickly spread when they are well-known or become viral. For food truck operators, even if are already on social media, you need to integrate YouTube in your marketing plan.

Chapter 9: Menu

For owners of food trucks the most important thing to be successful is having a variety of tasty dishes. It's difficult coming up with creative ideas that are simple to cook. In this regard we've put together some of our top strategies and tricks to create the flavor of your food truck's unique!

• Plan your menu simple. Choose three unique dishes.

Don't just stick to fries and burgers. Include other food items to improve the overall appearance to the vehicle.

• Serve desserts and savories. Don't be afraid to try some unexpected tastes and tastes.

* Choose the best menu item to suit your needs Keep in mind the kind of customer you would like to draw.

Try to use fresh and natural ingredients whenever possible However, don't compromise on flavor since you won't always get them in the local market.

* Provide a range of goods; this means you can provide something for to everyone.

• Employ a team of diverse members which will prevent food shortages, and will allow you to handle any issues that occur in the last second without jeopardizing your company's image.

• Make your truck look more attractive (or serve your food on the stationary table) with large white letters, and vibrant highlights (like umbrellas!).

• Display sample menus from your food items in strategically placed locations within the truck.

It is worth considering adding some "specials" to your meal plan.

You can show off your distinctive personality; give your vehicle an identity and a theme, and then decorate it to match (but be careful not to get too extravagant!).

The point is that there's no need to create a completely new recipe each when you come up with an entirely new recipe. Pick a recipe that you like (like the most popular food you've had elsewhere) and then make some adjustments to create your unique. It's not necessary to create something totally unique every single day. If you're providing what your customers love and appreciate, you'll be fine.

Create Your Menu

It is strongly recommended that before making any other plans you design your menu. This is the time to show your creativity since it is where you will let your food truck's distinctiveness shine.

The type of food that you're planning to serve at the truck you'll need to think about a few factors. If the food is exotic the customers will be excited to test it. If it's a standard kind of food, you already have a demand for the product you're planning to sell.

Consider what else are the options in the location in which you're planning to place the food van. It is difficult to stand out from other food vendors if there's already plenty of options. If you're looking to open in a crowded region, you should provide a distinct menu that is of the highest quality.

How to calculate your true costs for products and how to Price Your Menu in a way that is profitable

Three elements will determine the real price: ingredients costs cost, labor costs, as well as overhead expenses. It is crucial to accurately reflect these as they affect the pricing of food items in different ways.

Ingredient Costs

You must purchase ingredients that are of good quality and sold at a reasonable prices. The cost of every ingredient will differ based on the availability and demand of the product as well as the seasonal price. Learning what to look for in a menu and determine the cost of ingredients is crucial since it's the most precise method to figure out the amount you'll pay for every component in the food you consume.

Labor Cost

The cost of labor comes from two distinct sources that is your employees and you. The more you are willing to pay for labor and the more you're willing to pay your employees the better your menu will appear and also the higher number of clients you'll be able to serve. The cost of labor is a factor when the delivery of food to your customers. Food trucks at first glance may not appear to be an extremely labor-intensive enterprise. However, in reality it's. Labor costs can make up 40-50 percent of the price of a food item.

A good general rule is to charge what the customer will be willing to pay in exchange for services you offer.

Overhead Cost

"Overhead is a cost that's added to the food costs total which is used to pay for things like insurance and maintenance as well as rent, utilities and many other costs," says Katie Colwell. The cost of overhead is different for each food truck, based on their location as well as their size.

In addition, there are four pricing strategies that you can employ to ensure your food truck is profitable: lowering prices to compete and charging higher prices and establishing the concept of a tiered pricing system, and adopting a policy of customer satisfaction.

Pricing competitors' prices lower affects the bottom line of your business directly however, it also encourages customers to come back. If you price your food too low, it could result in losing customers, especially if the food isn't selling.

Pricing your menu according to the market price is a great way to go about it. "It provides the highest margin for profit and can lead to substantial economic growth" states David Goodman writer of "The Small Business Guide to Success: A Practical Method to Make money."

A tiered pricing method allows for a variety of prices for various customers. This means that items are priced differently based on the requirements of the customer and the kind of service that is offered. This will result in loyal customers. This can also make your food truck company more profitable.

You can draw repeat customers through social interaction or by generating income in the community you work within.

A customer-pleasing strategy is one that aims to try to make your customer satisfied by encouraging them to purchase whenever they come across something they are happy with. This will build loyalty and repeat customers.

The practice of charging higher prices is a tactic employed by businesses operating in areas with higher-end amenities and greater competition. This is a risky strategy because it could result in you having to be unable to retain your customers with the highest budget. If you are looking to increase your revenues but you don't want to damage the image you've built from the beginning.

If you're pricing your menu item be aware that food truck business is about the customer experience that they want Price points must reflect the quality of your product and service level. This will allow you to build a long-lasting customer base.

Tips to Make Your Menu More Delicious

You are able to be imaginative with your menu. Don't overdo it and you'll detract attention towards the high-quality of the meal. The goal of these strategies isn't to sway your customers.

Instead, use them to create the interest of your customers in your food. This means you will produce delicious food which means that your patrons will love eating it. Therefore, why not employ specific methods of psychology to aid them in making smart decisions?

Avoid Dollar Signs

You may dream of dollar signs all day however, you're not going to present them to your customers. Menus with dollar signs can draw the customer's attention away from food items and instead on the price. They should be focusing on the food item and its description, and not focus on the cost. Thus, you should list a number for the price, and don't include any currency symbols.

Prices at the End Differently

If you visit a fast-food outlet You'll see that all prices begin with "99." It's the standard for cheap stores. It's commonplace for stores to do this to make things appear more expensive than they actually are. Of course, you'll should follow this rule however, don't duplicate or copy the "99" style. This makes you appear cheap and your customers will think of you as a discounts for dollars.

Instead, you should end your price by putting "95." This makes your prices appear less expensive than they actually are, and you'll be able to avoid the impression that you're buying bargains for your food.

Avoid Columns

What do you first do when you notice columns? Your eyes instantly begin to look at features among them. This is the reason online service firms list their features in columns. It is easier to find prices in this manner. But, this isn't the goal you're trying to achieve in your menu. The listing of your top 3 dishes in columns can make customers choose the cheapest one.

If it's not a deliberate plan of yours, you'd like to stay clear of columns. Make lists instead, as well as let the descriptions promote the product.

Bracket Your Food

The only exception to column usage can be when bracketing your food items. Bracketing means offering different portions of the exact food at different costs. This is a tactic that large food chains employ frequently. The small size will be priced at five dollars, then the middle size for $7. The larger priced at $8. The size of each portion are visually displayed in columns. The large will appear three times bigger than the smaller size, yet it's still less than double the price.

People will typically choose the largest size as they'll find the smaller size to be more expensive. It is possible to do the same strategy with just two sizes, too. You can offer both sizes to your clients. The mere offer could make them think that the small is enough in order to please them. They'll opt for the larger to reduce the risk. If the larger size is twice as big and priced less than the multiple, people will think this is an incredible deal, and you'll find bigger portions with more frequent appearances.

Use the top-right-hand corner

Food truck owners don't use this method, which is an injustice. Instead, make sure to utilize the top-right-hand edge of the menu. You can highlight your most popular products or your top gross margin items. They'll be more popular and will earn you more money.

Make Use of Fantastic Photos

It's also something many food truck owners overlook which is a mystery. Customers like seeing pictures of the food they're going to eat prior to ordering it. Photographs that are great and highlight the images in prominent locations in your truck. If you print menus, put attractive images printed on them to attract more customers.

Avoid small print

Have you ever looked up the descriptions of product saw an asterisk beside it? Have you looked over the remainder of the webpage trying to figure out the reason behind it? It's a frustrating experience and reminds those who read legalese or intricate financial documents. On the contrary it is a time when people order food from you to unwind and have fun.

They don't want to be confronted with complex options with conditions. Also, avoid small print. Do not make your menu difficult to scan or read from the distance. Many people glance at menus to decide if they'd like to dine in the establishment or not. Do not fill your menu with food items that it's impossible for anyone to determine what's on the menu.

Be Consistent

If your menu is designed with the same tone and font, and your truck has another, and your website is the third, your visitor will be confused about what your services are. Thus, you must be consistent across all your channels. This is why it's useful to employ someone to handle your social media and other online channels. They'll ensure that the tone remains constant and the branding is in line with the current trends.

Don't be a bore

"Burger that includes cheese, lettuce." Or would you prefer "Smoked Burger topped with savory fresh lettuce and cheddar cheese?" The choice is evident. If these descriptions refer to the same meal and you'll probably think the second presentation is different from the one you saw earlier. It's a challenge to craft excellent descriptions, and to avoid writing lengthy descriptions. However, you should use as many adjectives as you can.

Create a picture of your client's mind. Imagine a scene that showcases your meals in the most delicious manner that you can. Then, write down the adjectives that pop up in your thoughts. Include these in your description, but don't go excessively. Avoid dull descriptions that appear as if you've made up something and then are charging for it.

Chapter 10: The Tenth Chapter: Grow

There are many options to grow your food truck company and grow it. The most appealing aspect is that you can make use of traditional advertising techniques including printed media, TV advertisements and radio ads to get the word out about your food truck. However, there are new methods to connect with customers, such as social media marketing, websites advertising campaigns and strategies for optimizing your search engine.

To address the initial issue to solve the first issue, you need to purchase an appropriate truck to your needs. If you operate within urban areas of big city, then purchasing an extra large truck that has all the facilities you could need will allow you take care of your clients and keep them satisfied. If your business is primarily based along national highways, purchasing the smallest truck will be sufficient.

If you're planning to start your own food truck store it could be a fantastic source of income and profit. In addition, many food trucks have recently opened restaurants as franchises for food.

The good thing about it is the fact that you don't need to think about hiring a seasoned chef to cook the food for your patrons. The taste of the food will be great as it will be passed down from one restaurant to the next.

Finally, purchasing a food truck will cost more money and has higher expenses than a traditional restaurant. It is a lot of work to prepare menus, transporting food from one location to the location and hiring a professional staff to cater the event and much more.

To get the most value of your money You must advertise your business using a variety of ways. Social media is the most effective method because of its coverage and the popularity. There are forums and blogs to communicate details concerning your restaurant business to other users.

Profiles of Food Trucks that are successful in detail, describing their operation Profitability, Scalability, and Profitability

What is the best Food Truck?

For a food truck to be successful, the food truck must create delicious menu items swiftly and efficiently, and also offer meals at an affordable cost. However, certain food trucks are focused on creating healthy meals or serving uncommon food item.

The formula for success usually is high-quality ingredients as well as an affordable cost. However it's all about the customers' experience. Whether they're served meal in just 10 minutes or 10 hours has nothing to do with the level of satisfaction they'll get when they try what you're serving them.

Overview of the Legal Consequences of Operating a Truck

Food trucks are in essence small eateries and are subject to federal and local laws. The health department oversees them, as well as local law enforcementagencies, and is also required to pay sales tax and sales tax.

A comprehensive list of resources including apps for locating Open Locations, how to build on social Media and Financial considerations

Sample Financials for Operating the business

The examples are for one food truck, with one cook and one server. The examples include monthly expenses as well as estimated revenues and profit margins.

Menu Planning

The most important aspect of any food truck's operation is having a well-designed menu. It's not enough just to cook delicious food. You also must ensure that you've got enough variety and quantities to keep your customers returning.

Operations and Management

Whatever the initial costs the food truck's performance will be determined by how well you and your staff control your own time.

The process of planning for growth that will occur

If you're considering going it alone it is important to ensure that in the future, down the road, you'll have the opportunity to expand to gain more profit.

Equipment requires

It's here that things get technical. The first thing you'll require is a trailer or truck. It's also necessary to have the power source to cook something and tons of ice and plenty of other supplies. Mobile cooks will also require containers such as pots and pans.

Marketing and Sales

The best method of gaining customers is through word-of-mouth recommendations from family and friends But you have to be more than relying on them. Promote your food truck on social media, invest in advertising, and ensure that you're available whenever people are looking to learn more about it.

Pricing and Packaging

In the end, based on everything you've learned thus far take a look at the way you'll display your food. Apart from the price of the ingredients, you need to determine if the way the food is prepared is something people are likely to buy. It's difficult to estimate the amount your food items will cost since it depends on the products you're selling at any moment. But don't fall into thinking that it isn't worth it since most likely, customers will continue to purchase your delicious creations.

Participation of the Community

Food trucks are a popular choice for people because they're interactive. Involve local businesses in your plans as well as with promotions that are special and appearances on special occasions you will build an audience. You could also participate in events that promote your community. This is a great way to get the word out about your truck.

How to Maintain Your Food Truck Moving Forward Start-Up Stage

I'm going to guess you've come here because you've got some ideas for your food truck venture and are wondering how you can keep it running. Let me help you how to do it.

Many think that all they have be doing is to park their vehicle and let the cash flow arrive but the reality is quite different. As with any small-scale business there are a lot of factors to take into consideration when operating the food truck. If you keep these factors at the forefront of your mind however, your venture will flourish.

While the market is overflowing today with food trucks Don't let that deceive you. There are some significant distinctions between a truck that's only opened recently and one that's been in operation for a few months. In the end, anyone can make an food truck. However, it's more than the simple act of building one. You must have customers actually come to your establishment, come back often and tell their friends the positive experience they had when they visited your food truck. It's not too the wrong time to inquire about your friends as well be on the lookout, but watch for warning signs while operating your truck.

For you to get the idea of things you should be looking for, I'll give you the actions you can take to ensure that your business is off to a great beginning.

In the beginning, you need to place yourself in the mindset of your customer when thinking about building your truck. What do they want? What are they looking for? to locate it?

When it boils down to it, the most important thing to draw people into your business is the signage. There aren't any random spots for food trucks. For them locate your food truck then you'll need to promote. Be sure to have a memorable logo, name and menu display with the entire price and description of food choices.

Today social media is an excellent way to spread the word out about your company. Utilize Twitter or Facebook disseminate information about specials coming up or events happening at your truck.

Another excellent source is word-of-mouth advertising. In fact, word-of-mouth is so effective that it's the most effective way for customers to keep coming back to your food truck. There are many instances when customers talk to their peers about their experience with the food truck and this can benefit your business more than any advertising.

In the end your company was one of the best when people only spoke about it. I'm not able to give you an exact method of making it happen however it's something you should be aware of.

Second, ensure that your truck is cleaned down every evening. If there is dirt or dust around the perimeter of your structure ensure that you clean it off. It's not long for people to spot dirt and view your food truck's cleanliness and unclean, and they might not return.

Also, keep an watch on your financials. Monitoring your sales every day will give you an picture of the amount of money you're earning every day. If you notice that the amount you're earning isn't keeping pace with the expenses of running your vehicle, perhaps it's the right time to cut back or find additional funds.

If you're running your own food truck and you've not taken the time to follow these guidelines then you're likely not to be out on the road for very long. However, don't let that deter you from trying. It's a fantastic opportunity to show others that you can accomplish anything with just a bit of effort. You could discover that this is just the beginning for your own food truck business.

If you're ever doubting you're in doubt, remember that even if your venture is not working at present the business could be able to come back later. The benefit of the food truck industry is that it's a lot easier to start a new one once you've established one. You're always able to expand.

You will stand out from the crowd

Food trucks are among the top highly competitive sectors across the globe. If you are looking to earn money, you need to stand out from the crowd. A good quality meal and solid customer service will only get you up to a point. If you're looking to get noticed and keep customerscoming back, you'll need some imagination.

Chapter 11: Management And Hiring

With food trucks You'll soon realize that there's often more work than two people could handle. If you're hiring employees, you'll want to start with an additional helper each time, based on your timetable.

The most crucial factor when you are hiring an employee. You need to be a well-informed employer to select the perfect employee. It is essential to follow the rules that are outlined in the "Small Business Administration" and be aware of the tax withholdings, wages and insurance in relation for your workers.

Further research on hiring is crucial to ensure that your hiring strategies match the requirements of the government. After you've followed all guidelines do you think about hiring outside aid.

When hiring, establish roles on paper to ensure everyone knows what their responsibilities are which includes you. Determine if you're going to be working with your customers or direct in your kitchen. This will help determine the employee's skills.

It is also important to know the food industry's mobile culture. There are certain values, customs and customs that have to be adhered to and observed. Decide on the type of culture and the environment you would like to operate within and then find employees who are a part of the same vision of success.

Finding the Right Kind of Help

Because only a few individuals own food trucks and they have to understand their roles individually, while working in a group. The staffing of a food truck is contingent on a variety of elements, with each staff member being assigned a specific role.

The size of your food truck as well as the volume of customers that visit will determine the number of employees required. Workers need space to relax and work the most efficient in their duties.

You must have a solid understanding of the amount of food to be prepared prior to deciding on the number of employees you want to employ. No matter how much you think you're able to do by yourself, there'll always come a time that you'll need help.

Food trucks require both back and front of house work, just as restaurants. Front of house (FoH) personnel handle customer contact and service while back of house (BoH) personnel perform operational tasks, such as cleaning, cooking, and possibly bookkeeping--depending on what tasks have to be done.

Front-of-house staff are responsible with taking order, writing checks, and taking payments. They must be aware of the work of the back of the house to inform customers of matters like the ingredients that are that are used.

The chef is usually in the rear of the restaurant and has charge of everything within the truck that serves food, which includes the flow of service as well as training and hiring in many instances. The chef is also accountable for cooking certifications, menus for the day as well as purchasing supplies and ingredients as well as the maintenance of equipment.

For bigger trucks, there's also kitchen workers responsible for preparing and weighing the ingredients. They can also clean, peel, or cut if needed. They can also prepare salads or other dishes that don't require cooking. In reality, most of these tasks can be completed beforehand in a commercial or commissary kitchen.

Controlling Your Employees

Although some managerial posts require employers and employees to be in more isolated areas and food truck owners are more comfortable with their employees due to the tight quarters of the food truck.

With this in mind however, there are still some fundamental methods to follow to ensure that employees are excited about their work. Begin by making sure you give constructive, positive feedback to the employees working for you. Feedback is the cornerstone of a great management.

Be sure to treat each employee as an individual, and avoid classifying them. You must ensure that each employee is respected in their work regardless of their role or the responsibilities they have. By doing this, everyone will be able to be more productive when working.

Perhaps the most crucial thing is to ensure the right training for all employees. This is not just a way to build confidence, but also ensures that all employees are working in a safe and efficient manner. Take a look at registering for leadership training to strengthen relationships in business.

Disciplining Employees

The process to dismiss an employee could be as difficult for you as it is for the person you're getting rid of. As per "The Wall Street Journal" firing employees is among the most stressful three tasks for any company's president, or manager. Don't worry about being alone even if you've not been in this position before. Even top executives struggle dealing with this.

Before you can get to the point to dismiss an employee it is important to ensure that everyone is aware of clearly defined rules to be followed for all employees. It is essential to establish the boundaries between an employee who is competent and those that are susceptible to disciplinary actions.

The way that rules are established and enforced is the basis of an operation being efficient. It's also easier to identify any weak links in the chain and could be addressed appropriately.

The rules you create must be fair and employees should be able to comply with the rules prior to starting their starting their job. Alongside distributing the rules, any possible consequences should be made clear to the employee at the beginning.

If an employee is found to have violated one of the rules stated Discipline may be necessary. The first step is to create an employee warning system , gentle reminders to employees of any rules or laws that was violated.

If the problem persists you should consider giving a more severe warning, possibly including a written copy of notice. If the issue continues to persist the issue may be a good the right time to think about the possibility of a probationary period that would involve removing the worker's shifts for a specified period.

Any warning, whether written or verbal, should be handled with a calm tone, and making sure to address any questions and provide support to complete the task in the manner it is supposed to be done. In any case, it is important to record the warnings in an employee's file.

If you are given a warning, ensure they are issued in a manner where they are considered serious. If there is a need for warning, address the matter with respect and with a serious attitude.

The termination should be the final step. Make sure the employee at issue is informed and that a variety of resolution options have been tried prior to dismissing them.

If you think a termination is impossible, be sure that the person who is at fault actually responsible in the incident before you take the final decision.

Important to have feedback from employees

One of the most efficient ways for managers to build efficient employees is to provide performance feedback, both positive and negative. Feedback that is constructive can fix small issues and also provides the opportunity to develop career for each individual.

Feedback from employees is a source of satisfaction, retention and also motivation. Feedback from employees must be given frequently, and should be given out of the blue when an event takes place, but sometimes it is with a set schedule.

If you do not provide employees with feedback, you may be missing a chance to further shape and grow your employees. Instead of waiting to inform the employee the reason why their work has become disappointing over for the last 6 months, you should ensure that you fix these issues at the start.

Be aware that providing feedback does not have to be viewed as a discipline task. Instead, try to be constructive and open to a discussion with the employee and take in their thoughts to encourage positive behavior and further rewards to aid the entire team to improve their performance.

How to Handle the Challenge

Food truck businesses are extremely competitive, regardless of the skills of your cook or your location. With the sheer number of food trucks operating, making a mark isn't easy. To gain an edge is about understanding the market and strategies that are successful and hard work.

In the case of restaurants, many owners try to find a place in which no competition exist. But, in the world of food trucks there will always be some competition to be had, which is why the best option is to establish an industry within a niche, offering inexpensive, special products.

There are indirect and direct competitors. Direct competitors provide the same services when they had two pizza restaurants within the vicinity. In contrast indirect competitors offer similar services, but with a greater variety of items including a different food truck offering the option of a side dish that can be your main meal.

Instead of becoming overwhelmed, think about keeping track of all your competitors frequently to understand their behavior and anticipate actions. After the contest has been thoroughly assessed you can begin to plan your strategies for fighting.

Begin by analyzing social media, and then reporting about local food truck operations. If a car appears reported in the news look into how this was the case, whether they have a connection to the industry or were introduced by word-of-mouth.

In the realm of the social web, you can find out what other people are saying about your competition as well as taking their advice and critique to improve your business. After that, you can talk to your clients in a casual manner to discover your strengths.

Contacting customers is the most effective way to find out about your competition. Find out why customers are purchasing food from your truck , and then take any suggestions to increase sales. Examine what they do not like and adjust it when it is logical.

Participating in related conferences and joining associations in the industry are great ways to stay on top of what's happening in the business. These strategies will help you stay ahead of the game which will make you the most educated person available.

Another approach is to communicate with your suppliers about more about the volumes of your competition. Although you might not get the information directly from a restaurant, you can ask suppliers to reveal crucial information that you can't find from competitors.

Then, conduct a poll. Find a way to gather data from your customers without pestering them. Consider reaching to them via social media or offering products such as clothing or hats with your logo for details.

Chapter 12: How To Survive In Pandemic World

Significant Changes that Food Trucks Must be following

The food truck industry is heavily in the grip of Coronavirus pandemic. Being aware of that the food truck owners must consider these changes to their businesses:

* Keep yourself in one location for the duration of the outbreak will help you stay safe from the more severe symptoms of the virus.

Purchase the generator that is powered by natural gas or biofuels and delivers the fuel every month. You can also buy gasoline that comes with an ultraviolet radiation sterilizer however, they are costly and are not always readily available.

Be aware of your local evacuation paths and remain clear from them during outbreaks of the pandemic. Streets will become crowded of people trying to leave regions where the virus is most prevalent This means that it's not safe to travel during these times.

* Put the UV radiation disinfecter in the food truck you are using.

* Make sure that your food truck is equipped with an ultraviolet disinfection device.

Make sure you stock up on canned goods as well as nonperishable items ensure that you have enough to last at least one month. Make sure to purchase at least 2 weeks worth of juice boxes or powdered drinks to ensure that you can incorporate these drinks in your diet for those who aren't able eating solid food during the time of the pandemic.

Purchase solar lamps that will provide light and security at night and set them in the area you'll be parking.

Do not use any plastic to cook your meals items; purchase the most food items that are already frozen as you can and stay clear of canned items. Even a food truck that is smaller can benefit from this method since it's less expensive than making use of frozen ice.

• Offer meals prepared by a professional such as sandwiches or hamburgers for customers who do not want to cook. If you're offering fast food salad bars are an excellent idea. it is also possible to provide desserts, such as cakes or Ice cream.

Do not accept cash payment for food as well as only take credit card, debit, or check-ins that are less than $100 at a time. This is because cash could easily be taken in the event that it's not secured when not being used.

What is the best way to ensure that a Food Truck still Earn During this Pandemic?

A lot of people won't want to venture outside in the midst of the pandemic. Additionally, many people who do venture out aren't able to purchase food items from your truck. Here are some helpful tips to food trucks owners on how to make a profit even in this epidemic:

You should freeze the food you're planning to serve during the outbreak.

* If you are able, buy shavings of the meat from a butcher, and then offer hot meals such as hamburgers and hot dogs. Avoid using lettuce in conjunction with these meats since lettuce isn't

sterilized and could be a risk in the event of a pandemic outbreak.

* If your vehicle has seating space, allow customers to order food items from your truck via phone, and then take it back later, once they feel confident going out again.

* Sell non-perishable items like muffins, cakes, cookies, etc.

* Sell things like peanut butter jars and canned goods.

* Ensure that your logo or color are seen from the outside of the truck, and ensure the windows of the truck are sparkling clean.

• Place signs inside and around the food truck describing the items you provide to allow customers to identify your truck easily when they spot your vehicle driving through the streets. Signs posted on the road will assist you in identifying the location of your truck when customers call to purchase items from you since they may not know precisely the location where your food truck is situated if they can't examine it to determine whether it's authentic or not.

Be aware of the location where you'll be parking so that you don't have to think about traffic, or get stuck in traffic.

* Don't take cash payments for food and instead, accept debit, credit card, or check-ins that are that are less than $100 at a time. This is due to the fact that cash can easily be taken when it's not secured when not being used.

* Purchase cups, utensils, as well as plates at nearby eateries that have shut down or are about to shut down because they are concerned about what could occur during the outbreak of pandemic.

Chapter 13: The Subject Is Marketing

Your marketing plan is likely to include different segments in it, and I'll go over them in the near future. Before we can get into the segments, you'll need to develop the template to organize the segments. By using this template, all you have to do is add in the relevant details that you will be able to quickly reference down the road. This is in contrast to creating free-form text plans that are hard to read quickly.

Marketing Framework

Here's the framework , or template, that you'll use to organize your data:

* Goal: Every food truck must have a plan and each strategy needs to work with one of your main objectives. Make a list of the goals that the marketing strategy is designed to meet.

- Audiences: If you have clients who are famous note their names here.

* Channels: Based on the information from the previous two points, determine which channel is most appropriate for your needs. If you want to attract people to the location of an event and you know that some famous people will be in attendance at this festival what platform will they use? "Instagram" is most well-known, but it is the case that in this case,"TikTok" is also a good option. What do you think? Would "Twitter" be a good choice? You could brainstorm ideas using this method.

The Timeline: How soon do expect to reach your objectives? Are there any major milestones that you would like to achieve? When do you plan to hit them?

* Metrics What are the primary indicators you'll employ to measure the progress you've made towards your target? You should ensure that they are easily measured and not intended to increase your self-esteem. If you can locate them, make sure you include the base measurements for each

metric, so that you can evaluate your performance against them. If, for instance, you're using paid advertisements What's a good Click-through Rate (CTR?) The exact figure varies however, there are general averages that you can use to gauge your performance.

• Responsibilities: Which employee should perform the tasks associated with this section? What is the particular job for each worker? Note their names and also. If you employ employees, this will make it simple for them to know what your expectations are.

* Budget: What amount will you allocate to this specific item? What is the best way to measure the ROI of your investment? In the case of certain marketing strategies it's difficult to calculate how effective your return on investment (return of investment). Think about implementing a feedback program to your clients. When they place an order, let them provide feedback on how they discovered you. Another option is to offer discounts or checkout codes that are different to different platforms and methods. Customers will

utilize these codes as well, and you can monitor their use quickly. Divide the revenue you earned through each of the channels by amount you spent on it and you'll be able to get an accurate ROI measure.

I'd like you to know that you don't need to be aware of all these elements beforehand or even all of these elements included in the template. It's your decision and you should decide what makes sense to you. If you feel that a text-free approach prefers to an organized piece like this, do it. So long as you have the ability to track the ROI of this investment, the work is worth it. These are the methods you can employ to market your company. These are individual parts of your marketing strategy.

Media/PR Remarks

Journalists are always in the looking for stories that are interesting and compelling. Consider the things that make your food truck unique and present this idea to journalists. There are many ways to make your food make your mark in their eyes. The most reliable method is to give a human perspective. Have you ever flipped to the cable news and seen a positive report? Journalists are prone to eat these stories. For you it could be that is related to you or an thing on your menu. Perhaps your grandmother influenced an item that's been long forgotten, or maybe it's a fresh take on it. Everyone has stories to tell, so take a moment to think about the elements that make your story unique.

The other strategy is to learn the current trends. The environment is of paramount importance in the present, so you should present this information to journalists. Maybe that your containers for food are compostable or your food is produced locally or from local suppliers, and the list goes on. Attracting customers with the latest trends is always an effective marketing strategy.

Certain cooking techniques or food trends are great to learn about. Are you aware of the excitement was felt in New York City when the Cronut first came out? Every bakery that was in the city took advantage of it, not even the initial creator of the sweet. Although it was a fabricated occasion There are local trends that captivate people the same way. Make use of this.

Make sure that your marketing strategy isn't just something you put in place when you launch. It's a continuous strategy. You should concentrate on your employees as well as at your clients. Maybe there's a customer who comes back constantly. Learn more about them. You never know if they have an interesting story to help you gain more attention? It could happen in indirect ways also.

For instance it was reported in a recent report on an 89-year old pizza delivery man who was given the sum in the amount of $20,000 from one of his frequent customers. The client was thrilled to order from Papa John's, the nearby Papa John's where the driver was employed. Although the story only mentioned the restaurant in a non-specific way but you can be sure that the restaurant saw an increase in customer traffic because of the account. Always keep an eye out for opportunities like this.

Events

Special events can be a opportunity to mine gold for your. They attract thousands of people and all require food. If you've been to the music festival you're aware of the types of crowds you'll see. It's also an excellent opportunity to make your name viral. Make a calendar of events prior to the event to be aware of the time to start preparing for it. Every event comes with its own marketing method which is why you'll need to determine the best way to promote each event.

The creation of a unique hashtag for an event and urging your clients to use it is a great method to increase follower numbers and increase engagement. Another method to consider is to join forces together with food sellers during the event. If someone is selling items that are similar to your own, you could team together and offer a discount on the total purchase. It is important to determine the margins with the other owner but these kinds of partnerships are frequent. In fact, you'll see other owners calling you after you register for your first event.

You might also think about creating unique packaging for your event and encourage your customers to make use of it in creative ways to promote your company. Give away prizes or incentives to users to share their experiences and interact with your social media accounts. For instance the hashtag mention, will give them a free soda. Food trucks often have screens outside to display the most recent tweets as well as Instagram mentions. The possibility of seeing themselves on the screen can be a good incentive for customers to connect with you via social media.

You can make giveaways and encourage people to sign up by putting up landing pages on special occasions. This is especially relevant when you own a company connected with your truck's food service. Food truck vendors often operate catering services as well. If you know someone who has an event or wedding due to be held, you could invite them to sign up for your service via your link. A different option would be to give your customers the chance to win a week's worth meals for a price.

It's not easy to achieve without the proper delivery system however, you could give seven meals a day for the rest of the week. Then, request that they sign up and pay on an online landing page or your website. You will not only be able to capture their email addresses for future communication and follow-up, but you'll also get orders for the coming week. Add this to the normal profits you'll earn this will provide an enormous boost for your business. When your business is growing it is possible to use your food truck during events to create secondary businesses that will be sustained by this method. This creates two streams of income for you which is something most people who own food trucks would be dying for.

Branding

It is a thing you must to take care of in the first place, but the method to do it are different. Food trucks give you the chance to distinguish yourself from the rest. A majority of food trucks choose vinyl wrap. This isn't an easy DIY technique, which means you'll have to engage an outside service, which is expensive. It's a good thing that you'll be able to create uniformity across the channels you use for marketing. If you've got an intricate logo or artwork that you want to wrap around your truck, then vinyl wrapping it might be the most effective way to move. Another alternative is to paint it by hand. It's a lengthy process and the majority of proprietors of food truck are not professional artists. It's therefore unlikely to paint more than some basic designs. The good thing is that it's not expensive. It also gives you the chance to make your mark in the crowd. It is possible to hire an artist from your area to decorate your truck and then use the publicity to draw attention to your business. If your food item is local as well as has an eco-friendly focus for it, it can be the ideal method of bringing customers to your business. It is possible to choose both strategies for practical reasons. This method may not work for everyone. However, you can think about having talented artists paint your vehicle every week or once a month. This gives them publicity for free as well as keeps your vehicle looking new. There are some logistical issues for this but definitely worth trying.

Apps

Food apps provide you with the chance to build your client base, and you might want to consider creating an app of your own. There is no need to pay developers to develop your app by hand. You can go for what's known as a white-label service. The client will be provided with the template application that will do everything you need. All you have to do is the branding you want as well as other elements you'd like to change. The app you choose to use is sent to you and appears and feels exactly like the one you've created. "TouchBistro" can be a good example of a white label app service. The greatest benefit of the App is the Analytics tool will be provided. These apps let you monitor your customers' actions through your app, so that you'll be able make better choices in regards to marketing, as well as other aspects and functions of your business.

Website

Every business should have a website nowadays. It's possible to think that with an application and a social media profile it isn't necessary to have websites. This is not the right approach to adopt. Web presence is like purchasing an investment property in the present. If you decide to stake out your web presence you can claim it to be yours. Your website will also be with a blog and you can utilize this to increase customers to your website organically. This is accomplished through SEO (search engine optimization). SEO requires time to really get going however once it is it, it's an excellent way to drive free traffic. You could even transform your website into a shop and sell your sauces and menu items via it. For instance, your customers may be asking questions about the specific sauces that you use for your food. Make it into a bottle and then sell it on your website! It's not possible to do this through your social media accounts. It is possible to list what you serve on your site You can also provide locations and recipes as well as conduct polls and also publish your event calendar. Maintaining a well-maintained blog is a great way maintain "Google" satisfied and will recommend your site to people. There are numerous ways to earn money through a website. You can, for instance, advertise on your site when your page's views are sufficient. Then, you could think about publishing a cookbook that has your recipes. Other merchandise like T-shirts, hats and hoodies are very popular too. The first step is to create your own website. Set it up and the opportunities to monetize will be taken care of. As your company grows you should keep coming back to this section of your strategy and continue to update it.

Scale your business

After you've been running your business for a while and built an established customer base, you could decide it's the right time to build your business immediately. The plan for the creation of the brand, as well as its design during the initial phase must be discussed with you as well as your team. Do you think that more trucks will lead to expansion? Do you want to set up an establishment with bricks and mortar? What are the goals of the timing of debt repayment to ensure that your company gets the security it requires while also paying investors on time? Do you think a franchise model is an option? There are many ways to profit from your success brand. However, none should be considered until you've been operating for at the least a year unless demand immediately surpasses the cost. There are some reasons to this. As the business's owner of the business, you must know whether the success of your truck depends on the season's traffic or weather like having extremely busy and long-running periods. The second thing to do is give your business the chance to grow with all the errors, issues and problems that could be unforeseeable in the beginning. This will allow you to prepare for these issues during the period of expansion. In addition, early development could cause a deficiency of capital that could harm the health of a company otherwise. This is why you must be savvy.

Create Your Brand

Your company's brand should be noticeable and distinctive to you, either from your truck or otherwise to ensure that customers will be able to immediately see and be able to recognize the services you provide. It's the impression you're trying to convey to the client that attracts customers to your company. Your brand's identity is more than a logo wraps for the truck.

The logo is crucial however, all of your branding products should match one another and contribute to your business and its offerings being more easily recognized. The top designs are simple to remember and easy. They are the ones you don't have to explain are among the top brands. If someone sees the logo, they'll instantly know what the food truck's mission is. The top brands also have an appeal to the market you are targeting. The connection you create will be based on the demographics as well as psychographic characteristics.

It is important to understand what their emotional triggers are and incorporate that into the brand's personality. The nature of your brand's identity should be uniform. The trucks should also be decorated with wraps or signage if you have several trucks.

Here are a few ways you can advertise your food truck company:

Decorating

When you are preparing your truck section, you'll need to consider the factors previously mentioned. The truck itself is the greatest advertising you can get for your vehicle. Take into consideration how it's at a distance when you design the exterior of your truck as well as how it's seen from close.

Food trucks usually feature a single, intense color to be observed from the distance. Choose a hue that is sure to make a statement. Consider other famous colors of the food trucks that are in your town. The color you'd like to have most likely isn't currently being used. Also, if it becomes dirtier, you should consider the way your color might appear. Certain shades of paint stand up to a little small amount of dirt better more than others.

Menu Board

One of the most important methods you can communicate with your customers is through your menu. The menu should not only be able to communicate your menu's offerings in a clear and effective manner however, it also provides an opportunity to communicate your company's image. The menu must be appealing and clear visually. Be sure that the font of the text is big enough to be read from an extended distance by your guests. Take note of how the menu changes through your eyes, and where it stays. Be aware of your pricing psychology. How can more side dishes or drinks be offered? These should be given special attention if you are selling special products.

Website

The presence of your website on Web will be a crucial element of how your customers interact with your brand on a general level. When you design your site, ensure that it promotes your brand image and contains the most important information that is easily accessible to your clients.

Expand Your Fleet

The decision to broaden the scope of your food truck empire must be based on careful consideration of various aspects such as your company's financial situation, the logistical aspects that go into making the shift, and also the level of your psychological readiness. You should consider the factors listed in the following sections prior to the expansion of your enterprise. The addition of a second truck to your business will mean you're going need to purchase more items. It is possible to receive lower prices on everything, in large quantities, however when you increase your buying quantity, you might be able get lower costs for everything, which includes the ingredients for your menu and packaging.

A truck could also place you in a stronger position to protect your company against the price-cutting of your competitors. You might be able to sell more products as you expand to new markets. This increase in sales could assist in compensating for lower profits per unit.

You must carefully consider the economic implications of any expansion, and determine if your cash flow is sufficient to support the investment. It is crucial to know the best way to get the funds to finance an additional truck, a brand new inventory, and a bigger personnel. If your plan has shown (by an excellent top line) that there is a demand it is the best time to increase your staff.

Franchising

You could also grow your business by franchising. The term "franchising" refers to an arrangement in which the sole or exclusive retailer of the trademarked item or service grants exclusive rights to local sales to retail stores in exchange for a fee and agreeing to established operating procedures. If you decide to expand your business through franchising, franchisees will pay you a franchise fee to use the trademark you have and your menu. It is possible that you will need to provide assistance and education for your franchisees in order to operate food trucks similar to yours. In the future, they could continue to pay you 4-8 percent royalty on the sale.

Chapter 14: Monitor Costs

Starting a business can be costly It is essential to determine how you can cover the initial costs before you can move your food truck concept off the sketchboard and out on the streets. It's no secret that planning menus and designing your food truck are to be the "fun" aspect of this venture. Although it is enjoyable operating food trucks, be aware that it's an actual business and must be treated as such. The appearance of a food truck can be misleading and beginning a food truck company is similar to starting any other restaurant, except for the flexibility and lower initial cost. This isn't a fast-track to riches! It requires a lot of time and commitment to succeed and thrive in this business.

Pay Attention to your cash flow

To succeed for success, you must be aware of your money flow. This can be achieved by ensuring proper pricing and making smart purchases of supplies. Additionally, you must be aware of costs. There is no fixed cost for starting a gourmet restaurant truck business. Each truck's food is different and requires different specifications. Begin by making an inventory of all the costs you could imagine. Don't be surprised when your expenses are rising quickly. It is important to determine the cost to prepare each dish.

This is essential since, in the beginning, it is important to establish a realistic estimate of the sum needed to establish and run your company. Also, don't forget the accounting, legal and other financial costs.

Operating expenses

Another aspect of the equation is operating costs (or the overhead cost). Operating expenses are the regular costs to keep your business operating. It is possible to think of operating expenses as recurring monthly installments. Further breaking it down provides us with fixed and variable costs. Examples of fixed costs include vehicle payments, commissaries and rental of vehicles, web hosting, as well as insurance. For variable costs, such as components such as repairs, fuel marketing, and even special permits could fall under this category. It's crucial to estimate your expenses every month as accurately as you can. It is also possible to plan a bit more to cover the unanticipated. Costs that are unexpected can result due to last-minute incidents or repairs to vehicles. Remember that it will take some time for your company to be profitable. It can be difficult to watch your money flow out of the window without returns on investment in the beginning. The greater amount you invest in the beginning, the more time it takes to repay it. One benefit of food trucks is that it is less expensive to run operating costs.

But, you'll require sufficient capital for you to keep operating for at least 6 months or 1 year at the beginning. Research has shown that businesses typically need at least two years to begin to see profit. For many this is a long time!

Managing Food Volume

You'll need to be able to manage the amount of food you consume. Here are the factors that determine the volume. A large part of that is the quantity of food you'll need to purchase, and how much you'll need to cook. You will then have to determine how much you will be able to market. Estimating the amount of food you need can be a challenge. You can estimate your business's food intake at first however, only the experience you have will help you get better in estimating how much food to purchase and cook.

The constant challenge is working out the quantity of food you will serve at a function. It's contingent on the amount of food you believe you are able to sell. In most cases, you will not know until you're empty of your food. If you do end up running out of food items, you'll never be aware of how much food you could have been able to sell! This can be extremely frustrating.

Another issue is that you are only given an hour for selling your products since you're not open all the time like traditional restaurants. It is essential to be able to prepare food quickly and in a large volume. Another element that is important to consider is the right pricing for your menu. There must be an appropriate balance between the pricing. When your costs are excessive it will be difficult to sell food.

If your prices aren't competitive enough then you'll not make profits. The majority of food trucks sell items between $6 and $10 however some are more expensive.

Building Loyal Customers

To establish a strong reputation of your car, it is essential to offer a reasonable price. You can check the costs of similar products to your competition. Pricing your products at the right price is another ability that is acquired through the experience. Your location is a factor in determining how much your customers are ready to spend. The price in one place will differ from another city. Size of portion will determine the price you pay.

It is important to determine the factors that differentiate your food from your competitors. If you're charging more than your competitors, you have to explain the reason why it is more expensive.

Here are a few reasons why you could make more money from your food items than your competition:

* You may use organic ingredients or you may be providing side dishes not provided by your competition.

* The size of your portion may be greater.

Perhaps you're making use of imported ingredients. A gluten-free menu could be a reason to charge more.

The main point here is that if you're spending more than you're making Then adjustments have to be implemented.

The modifications you could make are:

- Reducing supply costs

* Get bulk discounts on your ingredients

- Adjusting employees' numbers

You can join a co-op or improve your marketing techniques. Once you've calculated your expenses decide how many products you'll need to sell to make it profitable.

The beginning year is expected to be the most challenging to make money! This is where the most adjustments are made. There will, of course, be some things beyond your control, for instance:

Weather conditions are not ideal.

* Event cancellations

* Health problems

* Car breakdowns

It's all part and parcel of business and each industry faces similar challenges. A lot of patience will be a huge help to assist you in the most difficult aspects of starting a business.

Budgeting and Accounting Tips for Budgeting and Accounting

When you are balancing your financials and balancing your finances, it is crucial to build a security net before acquiring new equipment or introducing unnecessary costs to operating your truck , and thereby bolstering your brand. Like any small-sized business there is a chance that you won't reach profit quickly. Setting up separate business accounts from the beginning will simplify the budgeting process.

Although you might not be able to hire an independent financial adviser initially, keeping an up-to-date budget can help ease the anxiety and stress that could arise from your budget. The reports of your POS system can help in this process. If your business grows or, alternatively, you have difficulty meeting your financial obligations you may want to talk to an expert.

Be aware of your strengths and appreciate your time. Even if your an ex- CPA It might not be worth the cost to put together quarterly tax returns. You could prefer to develop your calculations in an application such as Excel However, there are a variety of templates online that are designed to satisfy the requirements of small-sized businesses. In the first year as a business owner there may not be other options.

Take a look at all the demands you place on the time you spend as a small-scale business owner, and plan enough time off. We get it. You're committed to seeing your food truck successful. However, you can't do this if you're running yourself over the edge. Making a list of every single task that demands your time will allow you to recognize how much work you're accomplishing while making it easier to manage the various tasks that you have to complete.

Profits and expenses

While food trucks have the benefit of being able to move to the location where people are, the come with the drawback of breaking down. Even the smallest of issues require a trusted mechanic to repair the issue before they occur.

There are a lot of mechanics are on hand for all repairs to vehicles however, there is a smaller number of mechanics available when it comes to repairs for food trucks depending on the issue and the location. It is therefore crucial to find some trusted truck mechanics prior to when you have issues.

If you're looking for reliable repair for your truck, think about speaking to your friends or even rivals whom you can be confident in. Look up references to those who frequently use specific mechanics to find a mechanic who is trustworthy and honest. Also, make sure to check online reviews whenever possible.

When you're experiencing kitchen problems It's better to speak to the people you trust as competitors or even suppliers who might have someone to help resolve the particular equipment that you're experiencing problems with.

The aim of your venture is likely to be to earn money doing something you enjoy. A lot of people have a very imagination however they may not have with a solid business sense. It's not difficult to alter! The goal the purpose of Business

Shark books is to educate entrepreneurs on how to be successful in both business and in life.

One of the most effective tips available is to ensure that you're earning a profit and to invest that money. You need to ensure that you have the ability to ensure the wellbeing of your family and your family regardless of what happens to your business. Incorporating profit into every aspect of your business will guarantee this!

As we have discussed it is important to incorporate profit into the prices you charge. It is also important to incorporate an effort to incorporate your earnings into the pricing. Profits are added on top of your earnings! There isn't a set amount but you can start at 10. If you can do more, then go for it.

As you close all your accounts for the day figure out the profit. Keep a tracker and, at a minimum, twice every month, you should deposit money into your savings account with high interest. This is the investment bank account. It is advised to save the money until you hit the two-year mark or when that you've got three months' worth of expenses put aside. You should plan for unexpected events in case your business gets flooded, or you suffer an emergency fire, or another incident that forces you to close, it is essential to keep that cash available.

It is recommended to invest your money after you have saved more than three months' worth of expenses or are past the two-year milestone (when you are able to get an acceptable loan). The way you invest your money is entirely up to you. Numerous experts agree that property is one of the most secure and most profitable investment. Some prefer a bit of risk and take a chance on with the market.

Making profits

It doesn't matter if a food truck was developed from the thoughts of an aspirant chef or an entrepreneur, turning money is the most important factor to success, and is often the reason they are in this field.

However, if you believe that the money is going to begin flowing in once you start, be thinking twice! Maintaining and operating an effective food truck usually involves long hours as well as a lot of competition and a myriad of legal issues that differ from state to states. You might have seen famous food truck in the town or seen TV shows which showcase the glamour of this mobile-food business. The examples above might be a cause for you to think what a challenge this could be? You're not aware of the effort the owners of these businesses needed to do before they got to where they're today.

Food trucks are the same as starting any other business. It's necessary to start from scratch. The first couple of years will likely be the most challenging you've had to work to make enough money to cover the initial costs.

Staying warm through winter

There's one hurdle food truck owners face for all gourmet food trucks each year, unless you reside in a warmer climate region. Food truck owners often admit to finding themselves in a bind during winter months. In contrast to brick and mortar businesses however, the amount of customers you can count on in winter is likely to decrease to nearly none. If your food truck's operation appears to be slowing to the point where it's unwise to open at all you can find a number of other options to ensure your business is thriving through the winter months.

Another option is catering. Instead of looking for customers during the cold months the winter months, you can search for events or clients to attract customers to your establishment. Advertise as a catering service during the summer months and then seek out cater for events and parties throughout the year.

Alongside celebrations and parties, consider working with offices and other companies to cater to the needs of their clients. Consider attending conventions or tournaments that require catering. For certain food truck owners, the winter months could prove more lucrative than summer months.

It is important to embrace the flexibility of food trucks. There's no reason to be stuck in one spot. Find businesses that require catering services or additional options during the winter months, and search for major events nearby where you can make use of additional options regarding unique and high-quality food items.

At the final point, it's your decision to remain open in winter. Many other businesses earn their profits in the summer time and put off winter. If you do shut down for winter, it is important to remain focused on ways that you can boost your business's earnings the next year.

Unexpected expenses

Similar to the main expenses of the restaurant, food trucks are not without other costs to think about. With the price of gas constantly rising the cost of fuel could add up to huge expenses.

When you are parking your truck for business, finding a lucrative parking spot could result in the penalty of a parking ticket if not vigilant. If you park in an unsuitable spot could lead to huge expenses as parking tickets can be running up to $100 or so. Some food truck owners view this as the "cost to do business" however, generally speaking it's not a wise practice.

Chapter 15: A Mistake To Avoid

Many one is considering entering the food truck market hoping to create an enterprise that they can expand and make money from. It's definitely an thrilling and well-known kind of business. Food trucks are making their way to the streets in the beginning of each month across the nation. Although the market is expanding, it's an unfortunate fact that no one of the food truck owners will earn an income that is sustainable through the business. There aren't any reliable figures regarding how many food truck enterprises fail every year, however certain experts believe that the chance of failure is higher than 60% within the initial three years of operating. It's roughly the same amount of time that restaurants fail.

Before you begin doubting the value that the food trucks business It is important to be aware of of the reasons for the failures. This way, warning signs are able to be identified earlier and preventive action is taken. There are many misconceptions or lack of understanding that people who are entering this sector. Some believe that simply being a skilled cook, they are able to successfully operate food trucks. Although being able to cook delicious and tasty food is a crucial aspect of running a successful food truck but owners should recognize that it's an industry that has to be treated as it is. It's not a company that you can invest in and hire people to manage it...at least not at the beginning. It requires a lot of hours and dedication to create an audience. Many of the growing issues occur in the first the years. In addition, the cost must be properly controlled.

The public isn't aware of how much work involved in the everyday running of food trucks. There are countless hours of preparation work, such as the search for ingredients, location scouting marketing cooking, packaging and much more. Most often food truck owners are involved in all aspects of their daily activities and need to recognize this. The mere requirement of time can cause proprietors of food trucks close down their business within their first year. But, it is important to remember that any business worth building requires time to develop and grow.

A good practice to get from smaller to medium-sized restaurants is to make sure your menu stays at the size that is manageable. The truck you are using has limited storage space, as well as kitchen space. A lot of items you offer means you will need to find more space to store the food items. If your food truck is themed make sure you only serve the most well-known dishes for the kind of food that you offer. This way, you will be able to be successful at certain recipes while maintaining the same quality. If you cook multiple unique dishes and orders are not consistent, they can mix with each other and create chaos in your kitchen.

The waiting time of customers could cause negative emotions towards your vehicle. Beware of dishes that take longer to prepare. Food trucks' customers generally expect speedy service, particularly those who have been waiting in a line. Furthermore that the more people you can get through an area, the higher the profit. A well-organized process, from taking the order from the customer until the delivery of the dish and your customer in a big way.

Chapter 16: Food Safety Guidelines

If your food truck's operations fail to be inspected for food from"Health Department "Health Department" your food truck will no longer provide meals to customers, and earn profit.

Keep in mind that not all of the topics we'll cover will be applicable to your state inspector's requirements However, you'll be well-informed of the requirements your business is required to meet in order to be prepared for the inspection.

The following aspects:

* The function of health inspectors is to protect the public.

Inspection types

* What are the things inspectors search for

* Examples of food inspection

Health Inspectors' Purpose the Health Inspectors' Purpose

The primary function of a health inspector is to safeguard people from the spread of food-borne illnesses. They are therefore ensuring that your business's operation follows excellent retail practices and that it takes preventative measures to limit the spread of the introduction of pathogens, chemicals and physical ingredients in foods made for consumption by the general public.

Different types of health inspections

Three kinds of inspections are conducted through Health Department: Health Department:

* Check-in prior to the opening

* Periodic, no-notice food inspections

* Temporary inspections for events

A preinspection carried out by the Health Department before a food truck is opened for business and regular no-notice food inspections are the same type of inspections with one exception. Food inspections that are periodic and no-notice are conducted to ensure that you are practicing safe food handling when serving customers. Temporary inspections for events are inspections of food carried out by the health department for events that last less than 14 days.

Consult your local health department for the procedure necessary to provide food. What should inspectors be looking for? Health inspectors will be inspecting your commissary or commercial kitchen along with your entire food truck to ensure the organization and application of processes. A health inspector told me that a health inspector could determine whether or not you've got everything in order by conducting an observation lasting 5 seconds about the way you're organized. Specifically:

* Do you have your food permit correctly displayed?

* Do you have a clean food truck?

Have you figured out where you can find your food thermometer is?

Do you know the location of your test strips (for testing whether the sanitization process of water is properly done) are?

Do you wear an apron and gloves that are single-used when handling food items?

Are you using an empty wash bucket (green bucket) and the Sanitizer (red bucket) that are filled with water?

* Are food items on your truck just 6 inches from the floor?

The majority of these things are not difficult to understand, but you'll be shocked by how common these items are for food truck operators who have no understanding of what they're doing.

Basic Guidelines for Inspection

Restaurants, Commercial or even Commissaries

* Handwashing sink

* Hot/cold water dispensers

* Soap dispenser

* Paper towels

* Toilet facilities

* Self-closing restroom doors

* Paper towels

* Soap dispensers

* Trash cans with their lids, as along with trash bags

* Washing dishes

* A 3-compartment kitchen sink

* Cleaning, rinsing and sanitizing your items

* Test strips

* Food contact surfaces

* Nonporous surfaces

* Cleaning solution to wash surfaces

Good Food Best Practices

* No contact with the hands with ready-to-eat food

* Washing your hands at the sink for hand washing, and not the dishwater sink.

* Use single-use gloves

* Cooking food at the correct temperature

165degF for raw poultry

Conclusion

There's no way one book could cover all aspects that is involved in the business However, I do hope you now have an understanding of the essential aspects to take into consideration in becoming a chef-owned gourmet food truck. Each truck is unique and the dynamics may change dramatically from event to event, from place to location and one day to the next. It is important to treat it like every other company, and with realistic costs and a strategic plan.

It is certainly one of those industries which you can learn a lot in the field and while working on the day-to-day tasks. It's helpful to have employees and partners who can be able to witness the successes and the chaos which takes place, to help each work toward creating a food van that is successful. The operation can be "fast and fast" when your food truck is well-known, and you'll need to change when you realize that you're having difficulty maintaining your pace.

Even if operating the truck isn't easy and you're not able to tell your customers you're experiencing issues. Offering excellent customer service is the best way to make customers happy to make them return to buy from you in the future.

This is a fascinating industry to work in and it's very enjoyable however, be aware that a food truck's business must always be efficient in order to make a profit. There's no other small group of owners that are as passionate about their business as the owners of food trucks. It's an amazing group of entrepreneurs who are supportive of each one another.

Finally, as the owner of a food truck you belong to an elite group of entrepreneurs who want to work with their hands and get involved throughout the business. This includes cooking technological skills, mechanical abilities and problem-solving as well as logistics, marketing and many more! The day begins at a twilight time and will end late. Be aware of this and create an impression on your day and the lives of your customers!

www.ingramcontent.com/pod-product-compliance
Lightning Source LLC
Chambersburg PA
CBHW050403120526
44590CB00015B/1806